PENNSYLVANIA MOUNTAIN LANDMARKS

Pennsylvania Mountain Landmarks

VOLUME 4

Jeffrey R. Frazier

CATAMOUNT
PRESS

an imprint of Sunbury Press, Inc.
Mechanicsburg, PA USA

CATAMOUNT
PRESS

an imprint of Sunbury Press, Inc.
Mechanicsburg, PA USA

For information about special discounts for bulk purchases, please contact Sunbury Press Orders Dept. at (855) 338-8359 or orders@sunburypress.com.

To request one of our authors for speaking engagements or book signings, please contact Sunbury Press Publicity Dept. at publicity@sunburypress.com.

FIRST CATAMOUNT PRESS EDITION: September 2025

Set in Adobe Garamond | Interior design by Crystal Devine | Cover design by Lawrence Knorr. Cover photo by author. | Edited by Lawrence Knorr.

Publisher's Cataloging-in-Publication Data
Names: Frazier, Jeffrey R., author.
Title: Pennsylvania mountain landmarks volume 4 / Jeffrey R. Frazier.
Description: First trade paperback edition. | Mechanicsburg, PA : Catamount Press, 2025.
Summary: This fourth book in the *Pennsylvania Mountain Landmarks* series contains many new mountain landmarks not covered in the first three volumes. Just as in those previous volumes, this one also explores the legends and folktales that surround these intriguing places.
Identifiers: ISBN : 979-8-88819-327-3 (paperback).
Subjects: NATURE / Ecosystems & Habitats / Mountains | HISTORY / United States / State & Local / Middle Atlantic (DC, DE, MD, NJ, NY, PA) | SPORTS & RECREATION / Hiking.

Designed in the USA
0 1 1 2 3 5 8 13 21 34 55

For the Love of Books!

Cover photo: These two upright stones capped by a gigantic lintel stone at Collumcille Megalith Park near Bangor in Northampton County is named Thor's Gate. Photo by the author. See Chapter 1.

CONTENTS

ACKNOWLEDGMENTS

I would like to acknowledge my appreciation for the members of the Sunbury Press staff who have made this book and all the others in the *Pennsylvania Mountain Landmarks* series and all those in the Pennsylvania Fireside Tales series possible. Those folks include Lawrence Knorr who designs the covers and offers advice as to historical accuracy, editor Debra Reynolds who checks my texts in a meticulous way, and designer Crystal Devine who consistently puts everything together and produces beautifully designed final versions. Without their expertise and dedication, the books would be of much lesser quality. I look forward to continuing my work with them in the future.

THE FOREST PATH

by Lucy Maud Montgomery (1874–1942),
author of *Anne of Green Gables*

৪৯৫৬

Oh, the charm of idle dreaming
Where the dappled shadows dance,
All the leafy aisles are teeming
With the lure of old romance!

Down into the forest dipping,
Deep and deeper as we go,
One might fancy dryads slipping
Where the white-stemmed birches grow.

Lurking gnome and freakish fairy
In the fern may peep and hide . . .
Sure their whispers low and airy
Ring us in on every side!

Saw you where the pines are rocking
Nymph's white shoulder as she ran?
Lo, that music faint and mocking,
Is it not a pipe of Pan?

Hear you that elusive laughter
Of the hidden waterfall?
Nay, a satyr speeding after
Ivy-crowned bacchanal.

Far and farther as we wander
Sweeter shall our roaming be,
Come, for dim and winsome yonder
Lies the path to Arcady!

INTRODUCTION

This is a volume I did not think I'd write, at least not for another year or two. However, my publisher had other ideas, saying he wanted me to add a *Pennsylvania Mountain Landmarks Volume 4* to the three-volume series he had already published. I had mentioned that I thought I might almost have enough material for a fourth volume but would probably need to do more research and a bit more traveling to get the remaining landmarks needed to complete that volume. He had no problem with that, and so I began the work.

It turned out I did not have as much material for a volume four as I had thought. Nonetheless, I had numerous leads to follow, and as I did so other leads came to me like manna from heaven. Many were unsolicited; from readers who wondered if I had heard of this landmark or if I had seen another one. And as they came to me, I found them to be real gems, and also of such interest that I knew I had to visit each one, just as I had done for all others in the series.

Like those other places, these new ones also seemed to call to me; to beckon me into the cool depths of the forest and on to breezy mist-shrouded mountaintops. I had to wonder what secrets might be hiding in those mysterious sites; what curiosities awaited me. And when the mountains call, I must go. On the other hand, as my readers might recall, I have stated that any writer worth his salt will want to visit a place he's going to write about.

I identified with that philosophy because I knew I needed to see the landmarks I wanted to include in my books, not only to take photos but also to get a sense of place and a feel for the local color.

In addition, there was always the possibility, as had proven so often in the past, that when visiting these places, I would meet some locals who could tell me intriguing human-interest stories or colorful historical anecdotes that surround that area.

I had obtained much useful material just like this many times, and I had also found that if the person to whom I was talking did not have the kind of information I was seeking, they would put me in touch with individuals who could provide it.

Those kinds of personal interactions have proved to be very enjoyable for me, not only because of the information received but also because of my informants' cordiality and links with the past they provided. Herein are numerous links just like that, but quite a few of them are far more ancient in origin than the others, because they connect us with much of the state's Native American legendary lore.

The reader will notice that many of the landmarks discussed in this volume have deep-rooted connections to the Native Americans who had settled this land long before the first European colonists arrived on our shores. Such connections are not surprising, however, when you consider that these landmarks are ancient. They predate the humans who first saw them; were here when humankind began to explore the dark recesses where they stand yet today.

Then also consider how Native Americans cultivated and preserved their own myths and legends, many of which were attempts to understand natural events that, to them, could only be understood by a belief that supernatural forces were the cause.

So, dear reader, keep those thoughts in mind as you journey through these printed pages to those past ages and to Pennsylvania mountain landmarks that are unusual and, in many cases, quite remote. I enjoyed finding them, writing about them, and as always, sharing them with you.

CHAPTER 1

SOME PENNSYLVANIA
STONEHENGES

Archeologists in Europe have been fascinated for centuries by ancient stone circles that can be found there. According to one count, there are 1,303 in Britain, Ireland, and France. Of these, most can be found in Scotland, with 508 sites recorded there. Then there are 343 on the island of Ireland; 316 in England; 81 in Wales; 49 in France; and 6 in the Channel Isles.[1] The surprising extent of these mysterious places is enough to stir the curiosity of anyone, but their dimensions are even more remarkable. However, nine of them outrank the others in terms of size.

The largest stone circle in Europe can be found at Avebury near the village of the same name in southwest England. It is one of the best-known megalithic monuments in Britain.

Others that are almost as large include the Ring of Brodgar, a large Neolithic henge and stone circle in Orkney, Scotland; the Callanish Stones, constructed between 2900 and 3000 BC and situated near the village of Callanish on the west coast of Lewis in the Outer Hebrides (Western Isles of Scotland); and the Castlerigg stone circle, built during the Late Neolithic and Early Bronze Ages, near Keswick in Cumbria, North West England.

Not to be outdone is Boscawen-Un in southwest Cornwall; a large stone circle consisting of a central standing stone encircled by 19 other stones, including 18 made of grey granite and one of bright quartz.

1. Aubrey Burl, *The Stone Circles of Britain, Ireland, and Brittany*.

The stone circle at Collumcille Megalith Park. (Located near Bangor, Northampton County, the park with its stone circle and other stone displays bring to mind the mysterious stone circle of Stonehenge in England.)

Competing with it are the Rollright Stones, a complex of three Neolithic and Bronze Age megalithic monuments located near the village of Long Compton on the borders of Oxfordshire and Warwickshire in the English Midlands.

Mitchell's Fold, another enormous Bronze Age stone circle, can be found in southwest Shropshire, while Tregeseal East, with its nineteen granite "Dancing Stones," is a prehistoric stone circle one mile northeast of the town of St Just in Cornwall, England.

Then there is Stonehenge, located on the Salisbury Plain in Wiltshire, southern England. It is without doubt one of the most famous sites in the world, consisting of an outer ring of vertical sarsen standing stones, each around 13 feet high, seven feet wide, and weighing around 25 tons, topped by connecting horizontal lintel stones. All of these are set within earthworks and are in the middle of the densest complex of Neolithic and Bronze Age monuments in England, including several hundred burial mounds.

Stonehenge has puzzled archeologists from the time it was first discovered in 1620 until today. Built by ancient Britons over 45 centuries ago,

Another view of the stone circle at Collumcille Megalith Park. (This place is an enchanted land filled with surprises and marvelous constructs of stone that are reminiscent of those in England)

the reason they did so is still unknown, since they left no written record. Likewise, the methods they used to construct it are an even greater mystery to those who want to uncover the secrets it hides.

The monument's unfathomable past has spawned many imaginative and wondrous tales that purport to have discovered the true explanation for its existence. According to folklore, for example, Stonehenge was created by Merlin, King Arthur's marvelous wizard, who used his magic powers to magically transport the massive stones from Ireland, where giants had assembled them. Modern-day explanations are just as colorful, with some claiming that Stonehenge is a spacecraft landing area for aliens!

Legends and captivating hyperbole like this are what bring people to Stonehenge today, and which also were the motivation which led to the construction of a similar place right here in the Pocono Mountains of Pennsylvania. However, this Pennsylvania landmark was not constructed by wizards, giants, or aliens, but by one man who was motivated by a vision he had when visiting the Isle of Iona, in Scotland's Inner Hebrides, and not far from the aforementioned Callanish Stones in the Outer Hebrides.

When standing on Iona's highest mountain, Dun I, one day in 1967, William H. Cochea Jr. fell into a reverie, perhaps mesmerized by the knowledge that there were once over 350 standing stones on the Island, along with numerous sacred oak groves. He was also perhaps lulled into a deeper dream state if he considered that the ancient Celts thought of Iona as a place where the veil between dreams and reality was especially thin, thereby allowing one's spirit to easily travel between the physical world and the supernatural one. Or, in the words of those ancient Celts, *"Heaven and earth are only three feet apart, but in thin places that distance is even shorter."*[2]

Then Cochea began to dream, and in that dream, he was surrounded by a circle of huge standing stones which began to move closer to him. The stones were clothed in ragged and tattered garments and looked quite menacing, but when he thought they were just about to crush him, they seemed to emanate love towards him, rather than hostile intentions.

Cochea was so affected by the sense of ancient Celtic mystique he felt when confronted by the stones in his vision, that he came back to America with a desire to recreate a place where people could experience the same ambience he had felt in his reverie. It would be a safe haven where visitors could meditate, find solace and peace, communicate with nature, and actually feel what it would be like to sit amongst the circular stones of Stonehenge.

It was not until 1978 that Cochea could finally open his Columcille Megalith Park on the slopes of the Blue Mountain in northern Northampton County. His dream of creating a mystical place that evinced the spirit of ancient Celtic tradition had become a reality and was an immediate success. He finally had his place of mystery and myth.

The twenty-acre park, with over ninety megalithic stacked stone constructions, including a Stonehenge replica, evokes an aura of a mystical land where visitors might feel transported back to a time when ancient Druid priests performed their ceremonies and rituals in places just like this. This land of enchantment, as it can so credibly be described, has several miles of hiking trails, and those who walk them cannot be faulted if they sometimes wonder, if around the next bend in the trail they might actually see a group of Druids chanting their ancient incantations.

2. https://celticcommunity.wordpress.com/distinctives/celtic/thin-places/.

More upright stones in a stone circle at Collumcille Megalith Park

These two upright stones capped by a gigantic lintel stone at Collumcille Megalith Park, also shown on the front cover, near Bangor in Northampton County is named Thor's Gate. The stones came from local quarries, but look like they could have been imported here from England's Stonehenge since this construction is so similar to the upright stones and lintels that can be seen at that iconic place.

Stone fences and upright stones along Rishel Hill Road, Centre County. The local farmer who is creating this ongoing display, describes it as a "work of art", and it does add to the appeal of this country road.

A Stonehenge-like circle along Rishel Hill Road, Centre County

These thoughts would no doubt be invoked by the stones themselves, which weigh as much as 45 tons, stand up to twenty feet high, and date back 3.6 billion years. Imaginations are also no doubt fired when hikers pass under Thor's Gate, two enormous standing stones supporting a massive lintel. Likewise, the area called the Faerie Ring probably has the same effect, as would the hike through the Lands of the Water Lords.

Perhaps the large stone structures found in Columcille Megalith Park inspire its visitors to create massive stone presentations of their own that are just as impressive. There are reasons that this might be the case. For example, those who use stones to build stone walls, fireplaces, or similar constructs, this author included, may sometimes feel a kinship with ancient builders who got the same satisfaction from their stone labor and stone displays.

Then too, there is a permanency to those final constructions; a knowledge that they may well last far beyond the life of the person who built them. And finally, there is the artistic element to consider. The arrangements made with the stones may be another way for a creative person to display their talents; to get satisfaction in creating something that can be enjoyed by others. It would certainly seem that it was this artistic motivation that inspired one gentleman to create another Stonehenge-type display in Centre County.

One of my favorite routes from my apartment building, which sits above the beautiful Spring Creek Canyon country in Benner Township, Centre County, to the small village of Pleasant Gap is Rishel Hill Road. This little side road skirts several farm fields and provides some panoramic views of woodlands and mountains. I always prefer these less-traveled byways and so use them whenever I can.

Since I was quite familiar with the scenery along Rishel Hill Road, I was taken aback one day when I noticed some remarkable stone fences and upright stones decorating the landscape. Over time these wonderful displays became larger and more numerous, to the point where curiosity got the best of me, and I had to stop at the nearby farmhouse to inquire as to who was building them and why.

Much to my delight, the young lady who answered my knocks on the farmhouse door was quite hospitable and informative. She said her father

Another Stonehenge-like circle along Rishel Hill Road, Centre County

was the creator of the stone displays and thought that he'd be happy to answer my questions. She called him on her cellphone and explained that someone wanted to talk to him about his creations.

He was delighted that someone was interested, and so I trudged up to an impressive fence of upright stones on a nearby hilltop. The long row of rocks skirted the edge of a cornfield, and as I stood there admiring them, I saw a bulldozer heading across the field and coming towards me. Soon the dozer stopped, and its driver got out, walked up to me, and introduced himself. He was the young lady's father and said he was the one who set up the stones.

It is a work in progress, he explained, and he is doing it as artwork; to improve the look of the place and to make the area more interesting to those who pass through here. The boulders he is using come from large piles of landfill hauled in from excavation sites in State College where high-rise apartment buildings are being built at a rate that will soon transform the State College skyline into one that resembles that of a large city.

He intends to keep farming his fields and to preserve his farm, and so his creations should be around for some time. They will, perhaps, even inspire others with the same artistic inclinations to create similar sites on their own properties. In the meantime, I will continue to appreciate the Rishel Hill Road stone displays and look forward to new ones as they appear.

NOTE: Readers may wonder about the origin of the word Columcille included in the name of the megalithic park discussed in this chapter. According to one source, Iona was part of the Gaelic kingdom of Dai Riata, and the site of a highly important monastery during the early Middle Ages. It was founded in 563 by the monk Columba, who is thought by some to have been exiled from his native Ireland. He was also known as Colm Cille, and that name is no doubt the inspiration behind the name of the park on the Blue Mountain in Northampton County.[3]

LOCATIONS:
Columcille Megalith Park is located at 2155 Fox Gap Road, Bangor, PA 18013
Rishel Hill Road is located off Benner Pike (Route 150) halfway between Bellefonte and State College, Pa. It is Township Road 532.

DD GPS COORDINATES:
Columcille Megalith Park: 40.926918 -75.202266
Rishel Hill Road: 40.87745 -77.77516

DRIVING DIRECTIONS:
Columcille Megalith Park:
Take Exit 307 (Pa-611S) off Route 80 toward PA-191. Follow PA-611S to PA-191S/ Bangor Mountain Road. Follow PA-191S, taking a left onto Fox Gap Road. The Park is on the left side of this road.

Rishel Hill Road: See Locations above.

---

3. Adomnan of Iona, *The Life of Saint Columba, Founder of Hy,* William Reeves, ed., 248-250.

CHAPTER 2

THE DEVIL'S CHAIR

Located along a narrow two-lane highway in Wayne Township of Mifflin County, there is a high stone outcropping that has presented a challenge to local climbers and nature lovers for generations, since it takes a steep climb to get to the top. Sometimes referred to as the King's Chair, it is understandable how it got that name when the rocks are clearly seen—preferably in the fall when leaves have fallen off the trees and off the bushes that grow around it. At that time the rocks are most exposed, and it is then that those who look at them from the road below can see the top of the rocks. It takes a little imagination, but the topmost pinnacle does resemble a gigantic throne or chair.

There is at least one other place in Pennsylvania that has a similar rock formation. Overlooking Clark's Valley and sitting on Short Mountain of Dauphin County, the huge stack of rocks here was named the King's Stool by early Irish immigrants to this area who were reminded of a similarly named formation in their home country. See the author's *Pennsylvania Mountain Landmarks Volume 1* and the chapter titled "The King's Stool" for more information about this marvelous landmark and the history that surrounds it.

Nonetheless, it is the Mifflin County landmark on its Blue Mountain which we want to discuss in this chapter, and getting back to that place, it is interesting to note that it is also known by another name besides King's Chair. When that second designation arose or what inspired it is not known, but it is this name that seems to have attracted curious adventurers

The Devil's Chair – a side view. As seen from below while standing on Route 103 South
(Taken by the author in June of 2024)

The Devil's Chair – 2024 frontal view. As seen from below while standing on Route 103 South

to it, and the name that seems to be the most popular when people refer to it today. After all, who would not want to see a place called the Devil's Chair? As noted, there is no clear explanation as to why that name arose, except perhaps for the fact that it takes "a devil of a climb to get up to it!"[4]

It is not an easy climb, and most are probably content to view it from the roadway below. However, the name still causes many to wonder if there is a story behind it as well. Other than the theory noted in the preceding paragraph, no others have surfaced, but Mifflin County is not without its witch tales, which, of course, always have a link to the master of the underworld.

One of these Mifflin County witch tales stands out among any others, and even though it is set in an area that's fairly far from our King's Chair, it nonetheless indicates that there were once beliefs along the Blue Mountain that could have led to its naming as the Devil's Chair. See Chapter 4 (Lewistown Narrows) in this volume for the old-time witch tale in question. On the other hand, could the King's Chair name be of Native American origins?

Mifflin County has its share of these kinds of old-time legends and folktales, but it is also an historical goldmine of sorts when it comes to its tales about Native American incidents and chiefs. Although aborigines never originally referred to their chiefs as "kings," they eventually began to do so in order to use the same terminology the early settlers used when referring to Native American figures of authority (see chapter 8, titled "Half-King's Rocks," for more on this subject).

During the times of border warfare in Pennsylvania, it was these chiefs or kings that typically encouraged and led war parties to attack frontier settlements and colonists. On the other hand, if legend is to be believed, it was a lone frontiersman of a much lesser rank who is said to have discouraged those attacks.

Although no doubt more of mythical character than a real person, Captain Jack, also called The Black Hunter, is celebrated in local legend and lore as a protector of colonial settlers in the Aughwick Valley of nearby Huntingdon County.

4. From a notation on the back of a postcard titled, "Newton Hamilton Pennsylvania Beacon Lodge Camp for the blind—King's Chair, ca. 1910".

As described by one early writer, the Wild Hunter of the Juniata (another popular name for Captain Jack) "had an eye like an eagle, an aim that was unerring, daring intrepidity, and a constitution that would brave the heat of summer as well as the frosts of winter.[5]

The foregoing description, and those of other settlers in the area that follow, were written by a historian who is known for his embellishments to and romanticization of historical events, and who therefore has to be taken with a grain of salt. However, in all these cases his descriptions perhaps match what the popular beliefs and tales about Captain Jack and his fellow protectors of the frontier were in those war-torn times. I therefore include them here.

So, with that caveat in mind, we'll continue with that same historian's claim that "In stratagem [Captain Jack] was an adept, and in the skillful use of the rifle his superior probably did not exist in his day or generation. These qualifications not only made him a terror to the Indians but made him famous among the settlers."[6] See the chapter titled "Jack's Narrows" in the author's *Pennsylvania Fireside Tales Volume 2* for more information and history about the Captain Jack of legend.

Since Aughwick Valley is where Captain Jack is said to have flourished between 1750 and 1755, and since that valley is directly to the south and adjacent to the King's Chair at the end of the Blue Mountain in Mifflin County, it seems reasonable to assume that his reputation would also have discouraged any Indian "kings" from leading their war parties along the Blue Mountain of Mifflin County as well.

It turns out, however, that among the settlers living in Mifflin and surrounding counties at the same time that Captain Jack was a *beau idéal* of the period, there were several families who were just as effective in curtailing Indian attacks as Captain Jack was reputed to be. Notable among Pennsylvania's staunch Scotch-Irish pioneers, and the other settlers who were in the forefront of the expansion into the wild and unsettled interior of the state, were several sets of brothers whose reputations as Indian fighters seemed larger than life.

---

5. Uriah J. Jones, *History of the Early Settlement of the Juniata Valley*, 136–137.
6. Ibid.

The Devil's Chair - 2024 close-up view. As seen from below while standing on Route 103 South

Among this group of men over in what are now Clinton and Lycoming Counties, were Samuel and James Brady, and the Groves, Peter and Michael. On the Blair and Huntingdon County frontier, the Beattys, Kriders, Ricketts and Moores, family units consisting of seven brothers each, were also fearless foes of the native American sons of the forest, and, in the words of an historian of the area, were considered "the most formidable force of active and daring frontier-men to be found between Standing Stone and the base of the mountain."[7]

At the same time that the Beattys, Kriders, Ricketts and Moores were defending the frontier settlements of present-day Blair and Huntingdon Counties, the Coleman family, including brothers Michael and Thomas, was living on the "cutting edge" of that frontier, near where Spruce Creek drains into the Little Juniata River, present day Huntingdon County.

The Colemans were known to their neighbors as determined and skilled fighters of all their Native American foes, a reputation the Indians

---

7. Ibid, 279.

apparently entertained as well, for it was believed they "carefully avoided" the area inhabited by the Coleman family.[8] See the chapter titled "Tom Coleman's Revenge" in the author's *Pennsylvania Fireside Tales Volume 5* for more fascinating glimpses into these times of border warfare in Pennsylvania. Likewise, there was another frontiersman of that same period and area whose reputation also afforded him some protection from warriors out for blood.

The Pattersons—James Patterson and his son William (both were to earn the rank of Captain during the French and Indian War of the 1750s) came to the Juniata Valley in 1749 or 1750. Here they built a sturdy blockhouse fortress to protect themselves from war parties and then cleared the land to plant crops for subsistence. All of this took much time and toil, and so to provide some means of sustaining themselves, they depended upon their rifles to procure wild game.

From the time of his arrival in the Juniata Valley and well into his old age, the father was admired for his shooting skills and considered by his peers as "the most expert marksman along the frontier."[9]

It was not a trait that went unnoticed by the aborigines who often came to the trading post that James Patterson set up at this same place. From his many interactions with his Native American customers the elder Patterson knew that nothing would elicit their admiration, and fear of him also, more than his reputation as an expert shot with his musket.

In order to use this belief to his advantage, the Indian trader set up a target a good sixty yards from his front door. Whenever his customers made an appearance, Patterson or his son would nonchalantly take down their musket and fire away at the target, invariably scoring a bullseye, or close to it, every time they fired.

The Indians, upon examining the target, would express awe and admiration for the shooters' skills. By using a scheme like this, the Pattersons were able to keep their potential foes at bay for several years, until the great disaster of July 1755, when General Braddock and his troops were soundly defeated on the Monongehela.[10]

---

8. Ibid, 201.
9. Ibid, 365.
10. Ibid.

The Devil's Chair - another 2024 close-up view. As seen from below while standing on Route 103 South

This historical diversion into the events of border warfare that occurred around or near the rock formation that is the subject of this chapter has shed little light on the origin of its being referred to as the King's Chair. Likewise, our conjecture that ancient supernatural beliefs may have been the basis for it to be called the Devil's Chair is hardly convincing either, but it probably has some truth behind it.

On the other hand, it would appear that the most likely explanation for calling the formation the King's Chair is that the towering rocks do resemble a monarch's throne in merry Olde England; a regal place where a king could look down upon his subjects. It must have reminded those who first saw it of that type of throne, and so they named it accordingly. A bit of a stretch, yes, but a plausible explanation nonetheless, and probably the best that can be offered at this late date.

LOCATION:

The Devil's Chair is located in southern Mifflin County near its border with Huntingdon County. The rocks sit at the end of the Blue Mountain where it butts up against the Black Log Mountain in Tuscarora State Forest. The towering rocks can be found just south of Newton Hamilton, near the small village of Beacon Lodge, home of a summer camp for the blind.

DD GPS COORDINATES:

The Devil's Chair: 40°34'02.7"N 77°32'33.3"W

DRIVING DIRECTIONS:

Follow Route 322 and take Route 522 South. Off Route 522 South take a left-hand turn onto SR 3019 toward Newton Hamilton. Cross a bridge over the Juniata River and turn right onto Route 103 South (Juniata River will then be on the right). Follow Route 103 South for one or two miles until you see the Devil's Chair on the left-hand side of the road.

CHAPTER 3

TWO LANDMARKS IN ELK STATE FOREST

Elk State Forest is one of Pennsylvania's largest, covering some 200,000 acres across Cameron and Elk Counties, with small parts extending into Clinton, Potter and McKean Counties. It is named for the large herds of native elk (or *wapiti* in the language of the Native American) that once roamed these same forests but were wiped out by relentless hunting until the last one was killed in 1867 near Ridgway (see the chapter titled "The Last Elk?" in the author's *Pennsylvania Fireside Tales Volume 8* for more details).

The forests here suffered much the same fate. Once an arboreal paradise of towering white pines and hemlocks, early lumbering companies harvested the tallest and straightest trees for use as ship masts and spars. To get the logs to market, the companies lashed them together into log rafts, which were floated down the Driftwood Branch, First Fork, Bennett's Branch, and other tributaries of the West Branch of the Susquehanna River, which carried them downstream to the boom in Williamsport. From there they went to shipyards in Baltimore.

It could be said, therefore, that Pennsylvania timber eventually circumnavigated the globe; but by 1915 the timber was gone; and the lumber era in what became Elk State Forest was over.[11] Once-thriving sawmills and lumber camps became silent, and small company towns became ghost

---

11. PA DCNR publication titled "Fred Woods Trail."

Huckleberry Vista along the Fred Woods Trail

towns. In place of an unbroken forest of towering white pines and hemlocks, the lumber companies left a scene of desolation, one described by State Forester Joseph Trimble Rothrock as Pennsylvania's desert (see the chapter titled "Satan's Handiwork" in the author's *Pennsylvania Mountain Landmarks Volume 3* for more details).

It was an apt description of the vast wasteland of shattered stumps, discarded piles of brush, and fire-blackened ground left behind, and it took another twenty-five years before President Franklin D. Roosevelt's Civilian Conservation Corps (CCC) began reclaiming and revitalizing it.

The lumber barons no longer had any use for the lands from which they had greedily harvested millions of board feet of lumber, without any regard for conservation practices or effects on wildlife; and so farsighted conservationists in the Federal government offered to buy it from them for pennies on the dollar. The Roosevelt administration, as part of their efforts to pull the country out of the Great Depression, also created the CCC job corps about this same time, in order to provide jobs and income for the many unemployed young men who were on the dole.

Navigating a slot canyon at the rock city along the Fred Woods Trail

CCC camps were set up in decimated forestlands across the country, with nine such camps created in what was to become Elk State Forest. The indefatigable CCC boys built roads and bridges; mapped and cleared trails; and removed brush piles and any remaining underbrush from forests and streams, fuel for wildfires that continually popped up on a regular basis, ignited by lightning and passing steam trains.

The CCC boys were charged with fighting those same fires; and on October 19, 1938, eight of them lost their lives when fighting a raging fire on a steep Pepper Hill Mountain slope, just north of Sinnemahoning. Today a small roadside spring, along Route 120 in Bucktail State Park, is maintained as a memorial to all men who lost their lives when fighting fires for the CCC.[12]

Forty years later a new group of young men carried on the legacy of those same CCC boys when the United States Youth Conservation Corps (YCC) was created to perform similar duties. Today the Pennsylvania Outdoor Corps is a similar organization that provides these same services on a statewide basis.

The inherent dangers of forestry work have not diminished over the years, as forestry worker Fred Woods found out when he was injured in a heavy machinery accident while working in Elk State Forest in 1975, and died as a result. State forestry officials, wanting to honor Woods' services, authorized the creation of the Fred Woods Trail, and in 1981 the YCC expanded some existing undeveloped trails and created new connecting ones to finish that task.[13]

The five-mile-long Fred Woods Trail is considered one of the most popular and scenic trails in the Pennsylvania Wilds country. It is also noted as a relatively easy pathway with a slight climb to several amazing vistas and equally impressive rock formations at the top of the Allegheny Plateau. Along this loop trail there can be seen three amazing panoramic views of the Bennett Branch Canyon and its Sinnemahoning Creek below: Water Plug Vista, Huckleberry Vista, and one more as you near Driftwood. There are a number of impressive rock outcrops and chasms that can be seen along the trail as well, and which are just as remarkable as the views.

As you near Water Plug Vista you begin to see massive sandstone blocks that form a cluster called the rock city. The jumble of boulders creates a number of small caves, many crevices, and tight slot canyons, one of which is over two hundred feet long and over thirty feet deep. Covered with moss, ferns, lichen, and even with large trees in some cases, the rocks seem to be out of place; a remnant of some Devonian Forest that once grew here.[14]

Regardless of their intimidating appearance, the rocks still draw people to them today, just as they did in the latter part of the nineteenth century and in the early part of the twentieth century. That they did so at that

---

12. Ibid.
13. Tom Thwaites, *50 Hikes in Central Pennsylvania*, 84.
14. Ibid.

A 1901 personal engraving with star in the slot canyon at the rock city along the Fred Woods Trail

An emoji and more initials (also dated 1901) engraved in the
slot canyon at the rock city along the Fred Woods Trail

Another personal engraving in the slot canyon at the rock city along the Fred Woods
Trail - this one dated 1908

A pathway through the huge rock city boulders along the Fred Woods Trail

earlier time is evidenced by some of the graffiti carved into the walls of the longest slot canyon formed by the rocks. Two of those carvings are dated 1908, and an earlier one is dated 1901 (see accompanying photos).

It seems that the many crevices and caves formed by the rocks would also attract wild animals of all sorts that were seeking shelter. Rabbits, skunks, raccoons, weasels, foxes, and even bobcats may have once been found denning here, and perhaps even a mountain lion or two. There certainly is no doubt that Elk State Forest was once home to these big cats that the earliest settlers called panthers.

Early records indicate that mountain lions roamed these same forests as late as 1857. An article appearing in *The Raftsman's Journal* newspaper dated March 11, 1857, confirms that statement, reading as follows:

"Killed—a large panther by Nelson Gardner in Highland Township, Elk County, on the 4th inst. [means "of the current month"], measuring 8 feet 6 inches from tip to tip. The panther threw himself from a limb, so close to Mr. Gardner that the claws

One of the rock caves at the rock City - perfect refuge for a mountain lion!

scraped his hunting shirt, but the dogs scared it up a tree again, where it was shot."

There must have been many episodes like this that occurred here, all of which were likely to have been just as interesting. Likewise, there were no doubt many human-interest stories that could have been heard here as well, had someone preserved them. There is one legendary account that does fall into this category, however, and it has been preserved in the written record, the story of the "Maid of Blue Rock."

According to local tradition, one of the earliest white pioneers to come into what is now Elk County was a man recalled as General Wade, his first

Impressive stack of rocks at the rock city.

Water Plug Vista along the Fred Woods Trail

Nelson and Mary Gardner. (He was the slayer of the last panther in Elk County)

name lost to the ages. He was accompanied by a man named Slade, who may have been a lieutenant under him, but this is unconfirmed, and his first name has also been lost in time.

On this initial incursion into the area now called the Little Toby Creek Valley, Wade and his companion Slade found an Indian settlement there. According to the area's oral history, Wade and his party had come to dislodge the Indians. That history does not disclose why this may have been Wade's intention, but it claims that on the slopes of Little Toby Creek there was a brief skirmish between the natives and the Wade party, and the Indians were easily dispersed.

If this battle did occur, it has not been recorded in any histories of the area, nor in Sipe's *Indian Wars of Pennsylvania*, but given the local legend of the Blue Rock, it would seem implausible. On the other hand, the idea

that there may have been an Indian settlement here is quite plausible. This area
was a favorite gathering place for the
vast herds of elk that once roamed the
forests here and which attracted Indian
hunters who tracked the huge animals
down and killed them for the meat that
was a regular part of their diet.

Local history does record that whatever his intentions were, Wade was quite
impressed with the locale, and, along
with his family and his friend Slade,
returned to the upper area of Little Toby
Creek Valley in 1798 to homestead.

James McCurdy. (Also born in 1816, he was a
contemporay of Nelson Gardner and was another
wolf and panther hunter in the wilds of Elk County)

Here they built their log cabins and settled into the hard life of the frontier.
However, after three or four years they decided to move down the valley to
be closer to the Clarion River, and so they built new log cabins near where
the Little Toby Creek drained into the river.

It was when they were traveling back and forth between their old and
new homesteads that they would often see a young Indian maiden watch-
ing them from her perch on a large sandstone rock on the hillside overlooking Little Toby Creek. When sunlight struck the rock at just the right
angle, the rock glowed with a bluish grey hue, making it stand out from its
companions on the hillside. Although "flittings" like this were tiring, the
sight of the beautiful young maiden sitting on the strangely colored rock
was a mystery that perhaps invigorated and intrigued the movers.

It intrigued them enough, in fact, that they paused in their trips up
and down the stream to talk with the young Indian girl and to get to know
her better. Although she proved to be quite shy, General Wade eventually
induced her to follow them to their new homestead.

The story has a Cinderella-like quality to it from this point, since it
goes on to say that the Indian maid, whose name is not recalled, blended
into to her new family so well that she became an integral part of it and
Mrs. Wade became like a mother to her.

The ending of her story is just as romantic, when it's recalled that in
1809 the young maid and Mr. Slade were married by local Chief Tamisqua.

Afterwards, it's also said that the young couple moved to what is now present-day Portland Mills and started their own trading post there. A fairytale ending to perhaps nothing more than a fairytale, or maybe a true tale of romance from the Pennsylvania frontier.[15]

LOCATION:
Elk State Forest is located mainly in Cameron and Elk Counties, with small parts extending into Clinton, Potter and McKean Counties.

DD GPS COORDINATES:
Elk State Forest: 41.51164, -78.21806 41°30′42″N, 78°13′5″W.

DRIVING DIRECTIONS:
Elk State Forest: From Lock Haven, follow Route 120 North to the village of Driftwood. Turn left onto Route 555 West and follow it to Benezette. Here is the fabulous Elk County Visitor Center with amazing displays and historical information about the Pennsylvania elk. Here also the visitor is often treated to seeing live elk grazing in the highland meadows. This site is also a good starting hub for explorations into the surrounding Elk State Forest.

FURTHER REMARKS:

1. An interesting aside to this chapter is the story of how Pepper Hill Mountain got its name. Perhaps a bit apocryphal, it's said that the mountain was so named when a pepper shaker fell off a table on a log raft when it was making a sharp turn around the mountain on the First Fork of Sinnemahoning Creek below.[16]

2. Although the Pepper Hill Mountain fire of October 19, 1938, claimed the lives of 8 CCC firefighters, three others escaped death and injury by finding refuge on top of a large rock near the mountaintop. As a result, it became known as Survivors Rock, and it is known as such to this day.[17]

---

15. John D. Imhof, *Elk County, A Journey Through Time*, 73; William J. McKnight, *Pioneer Outline of Northwestern Pennsylvania*, 498.

16. PA DCNR publication titled "Pepper Hill Trial System—Elk State Forest."

17. Ibid.

3. Elk State Forest remains a nature-lover's paradise to this day as well, with its six natural and wild areas providing over 65,000 acres in which to wander: Quehanna Wild Area, Johnson Run Natural Area, Lower Jerry Run Natural Area, Pine Tree Trail Natural Area, Bucktail State Park Natural Area, and the M.K. Goddard/Wykoff Run Natural Area.[18]

4. I find no mention of any Indian chief named Tamisqua in Sipe's *Indian Chiefs of Pennsylvania*, nor in Beers' *History of McKean, Elk, Cameron, and Potter Counties Pennsylvania*. Online searches also proved fruitless, except for references to the great Lenape peacemaker Tamaque, a chieftain of the Turkey clan also known as King Beaver. He, however, should not be confused with a chief named Tamisqua, if ever such a person existed, since Tamaque died in 1770, well before the 1809 marriage ceremony supposedly conducted by Tamisqua.[19]

5. In addition to the fabulous views afforded along the Fred Woods Trail, the Ridge Road in Elk State Forest has been accoladed as the most scenic State Forest road in Pennsylvania!

6. Nelson Gardner (1816–1890) and his wife Mary (1826-1873) are both buried in the Pine Grove Cemetery at Ridgway, Elk County.

---

18. PA DCNR publication titled "History of the Elk State Forest."

19. C. Hale Sipe, *The Indian Chiefs of Pennsylvania*, 305.

CHAPTER 4

LEWISTOWN NARROWS

Every time I travel through that section of Route 322 between Lewistown, Mifflin County, and Denholm, Junita County, my eyes are drawn to the towering peaks and shady gaps of the mountain to the south. The sight is an inspiring one, and a place people should think of when they want to show someone what mountainous wonders our state holds. The Blue Mountain, along the border of Mifflin County and Juniata County southeast of Lewistown, provides in my opinion one of the finest mountainous views in Pennsylvania, and so it always inspires me. Every time I see it, I wonder what secrets those summits and hollows hold; what stories could they tell if they could speak to us?

This section of highway, known as the Lewistown Narrows, had a bleaker and less appealing aspect for decades, eventually inspiring locals to refer to it as "Death Valley." They named it that due to the number of fatal automobile crashes that occurred here with numbing regularity. To accentuate the danger it presented, the grieving friends and relatives of the victims of those car crashes erected white crosses alongside the road at the exact spots where the crashes happened. Then at some point they also erected a large sign with bold white lettering that noted "You must go through Death Valley to get to Happy Valley," with Happy Valley being the name that locals use when referring to Penn State and its environs.

Then finally, public opinion, the death toll here, and a ranking as one of the deadliest highways in the United States, finally persuaded the Pennsylvania Department of Transportation to convert it from a two-lane

View of Bixler Gap on the Blue Mountain

highway to a four-lane, which solved the problem. Now motorists can drive through here safely and appreciate the rough romantic prospect of the Blue Mountain, with its rushing mountain streams, misty glens, Indian paths, logging roads, rocky cliffs, and impressive boulders of all shapes and sizes; a varied landscape which provides fodder for interesting episodes that may have once occurred on these lofty heights in the distant and forgotten past.

The rugged terrain here has to be seen to be appreciated, and the Juniata River that flows past the foot of the Blue Mountain adds to the mountain's charm and mystery. Enhancing that enchantment even further is an old ballad titled "The Blue Juniata."

Said to have been one of the most popular songs sung in the Civil War encampments of both Union and Confederate troops, it must have appealed to the soldiers because of its heroine. In flowery verse it notes, "Wild roved an Indian girl, bright Alfarata, where sweep the waters of the blue Juniata. Loose were her jetty locks, in waving tresses flowing."[20]

Along with Bright Alfarata's saga, the tales the mountain silently contemplates must surely include those of other Indians like Logan or

20. Forest K. Fisher, *It Happened in Mifflin County, Book 2*, 7, 44.

Along the Bixler Gap Road

Kishacoquillas who once called these hills their hunting grounds. Likewise, it must reflect upon early Mifflin County hunters like Clem Herlocher and Dan Treaster, who forged their way through steep hollows and rocky glens when tracking the mountain lion, the wolf, and the white-tailed deer. Moreover, it no doubt broods over how the lumbermen came, bringing with them their axes and crosscut saws to clear-cut the pines and hemlocks that are still logged off here today.

Although its timber has been and is still being taken, the Blue Mountain's stories are harder to harvest. Many have died with the older residents of the area, but some have survived, and it was my objective to find them, no matter how imperfect my methods might be.

Given the dark countenance of the Blue Mountain's undulating features, I felt that among the many stories that could once be heard here had to be those about witches and witchcraft. However, those tales are often not talked about at all anymore since they were once shared in hushed and fearful tones, and only with friends and family.

Much to my delight, I uncovered one such tale that seems to have lingered here longer than any others of its kind. The fact that it can still be heard today seems to indicate just how deeply the beliefs about witches and witchcraft remained entrenched along the Blue Mountain. Adding to the appeal of this tale is the place where it occurred; in one of the deepest and wildest gaps on the Blue Mountain.

Bixler Gap is almost an unsettled verdant paradise, with lush trees, rushing waters, zestful mountain air that provides a cool blast of nature's air conditioning in the summertime, rocks and boulders of impressive sizes and variety on its steep slopes, and colorful displays of white rhododendron and mountain laurel blossoms in the spring and summertime. All in all, a pleasant prospect, but not one that can permanently conceal a dark story that was once believed to have happened here.

It can be said that tales like this were once widely circulated along the Blue Mountain. It is also well known that the old-time witch tales always have a component that links the witch to the devil. Witches, it was believed, had made a pact with the devil, had sold their souls to him in return for magical powers that they could exercise when in human form. However, they could not use the powers for doing good. They were committed, it was whispered, to continually wreak havoc, pain, and suffering upon humans and animals alike.

One such reputed witch was the wife of one of the original settlers in the aforementioned Bixler Hollow, so named from the family that first built their homesteads here. Mrs. Bixler was known as a healer, and was often called upon when someone was ill, since her cures often proved to be effective. However, people also believed she had a dark side and feared her for that reason.

No one wanted to upset her because it was thought that she could exact revenge by changing herself into a black cat, and in that form crawl onto the house roof of the person who had disrespected her, and hiss one of her evil spells down the chimney of the house. The spell would immediately cause much pain and suffering to the residents, and many were those who said that they had been Mrs. Bixler's victims. Furthermore, it was believed that her own family was not exempt from Mrs. Bixler's devilish charms.

A story once circulated that recalled a day that Mrs. Bixler's son Jacob was heading to their barn and found a large black cat blocking his way. Despite his efforts to get around it, it would not move. Finally, he decided

Nice view of Bixler Gap from atop the Blue Mountain

One of the rock towers on the way to the Witch Rock

Water falls in the creek along the path to the Witch Rock

to kick it, but just as he was ready to administer a good swift kick, the cat jumped up and dug its long sharp claws into his face, thereby leaving bloody scratch marks.

This happened again the next day, and then again on the third day. This third time so infuriated the young man that he took out his fodder knife and cut off one of the cat's ears, whereupon it scampered off howling into the nearby woods. Having completed his barn chores, he then headed back home.

When he got there, he was startled to see his mother waiting for him with her hand holding a bloody bandage over one ear. When she took her hand away, he could see her ear was missing! She then turned black with anger, and yelled curses at him, seemingly devoid of all motherly love. When her curses ceased, he was transformed into a gruesome beast! From

More waterfalls in Bixler Gap (Scene on a 1912 Post card titled "Mountain Scenery, Bixler Gap, near Lewistown Pennsylvania)

that point on he was forced to live alone in the nearby mountains, ashamed of his ghastly appearance and shunned by all who saw him.[21]

21. Forest K. Fisher and Daniel McClenahen, "Ghosts, hauntings, and witches, oh my!" *Lewistown Sentinel*, October 30, 2021.

View of the Witch Rock that glared at us through the mists cast by the little stream coursing through Bixler Gap

Now, the tale concludes, on eerie moonlit nights when the night wind stirs the tallest branches of the trees in Bixler Gap, and the light of a full moon casts the restless shadows of those tree limbs upon the forest floor, you can hear the son's howls and his mother's maniacal laughter. Some say it's just the cry of a bobcat or the screams of a screech owl, but others aren't so sure!

This old-time witch tale is typical of that particular genre, and it certainly contains many of the motifs common in such tales, including black cats and a witch's evil spells. Consequently, there is no way to know what circumstances might have led to the telling of the Bixler witch tale. What is certain, however, is that before science and education eradicated these far-fetched beliefs, they were once widely circulated and firmly believed.

Artist's depiction of The Beast of Gévaudan." Between 1764 and 1767 a mysterious creature savaged the rural region of Gévaudan, France. About 100 men, women and children reportedly fell victim to what became known as *La Bête du Gévaudan*, or the "Beast of Gevaudan." It caused a worldwide sensation. Most people at the time presumed the Beast to be a wolf and many modern scholars agree, but others have suggested that the Beast may not have been a wolf at all. It would seem that the Beast of Bixler Gap, if there ever was one, was regarded in the same way. Or perhaps the French beast was a storyteller's inspiration for creating a story about one in Bixler Gap!

FOOTNOTE:

When meeting Paul Rowles, the young man who, through a mutual friend, had volunteered to be my tour guide that day, I did not at first realize that I had found the right man for the job. Extremely affable, sociable, and totally familiar with the area, he spent several hours taking me up and down rough logging trails on his four-wheeler just to be sure I got the pictures I was after, including some nice views from the top of Blue Mountain.

Just as I had thought that my exploration of Bixler Gap could not get any better, my guide asked me if I had ever seen or heard of the witch rocks. I claimed total ignorance, and off we went, soon stopping at the start of a narrow trail that followed a small unnamed stream. (Subsequently looking at Higbee's Stream Map of Pennsylvania it appears that the stream might have been Granville Run or a branch of Jack's Creek.) The stream name was of no concern to me at that time, however, because at that point I was more interested in seeing the witch rocks along the trail ahead.

It was a quiet hike, the silence interrupted only by the splash of small waterfalls as the creek cascaded over would-be rock dams in the creek bed. The mists from the waterfalls and the invigorating smell of chlorophyll from the shiny damp green leaves of the trees that lined both sides of the creek made for lung-filling breaths of wholesome air as we forged ahead.

Although the path was relatively flat, it was still not the easiest of hikes, since the trail crossed the stream on two occasions, and on the way back I made sure I had fashioned a walking stick from a dead tree branch to balance myself when stepping on the slippery moss-covered rocks to cross back over the stream. Nonetheless, the large boulders and numerous stacked rocks along the trail and on the mountainside provided an enjoyable diversion and soon my guide announced we had arrived at our destination.

There were two rock faces ahead, one on the left and one on the right. However, despite it being a bright and sunny day, both were in dark shade

Another artist's depiction. This one of a lone wolf howling in the darkness and looking for its next victim. Picture found in Henry W. Shoemaker's *Extinct Pennsylvania Animals* in the section titled "Wolf Days in Pennsylvania" (page 111)

because of the luxuriant foliage on the trees around them. The foliage that spring seemed denser than I have ever seen, due I'm sure to the heavy rainfalls we were having at that time, so it required a lot of imagination to see the witch profiles in both cases.

Nonetheless, I took numerous pictures of both silhouettes, but none of the photos turned out well enough to show either one of the witch profiles. I therefore am including only one of those shots, and to see the witch's profile on this one, you have to look at the black outcropping in the middle of the picture. It appears to me that the top part of that formation is the profile from which the rock was named, but some may see another profile at the bottom with what appears to have a pointed nose, forehead, chin, etc. Whatever the case may be, the rocks are so-named, I would guess, as reminders of the once popular tale about the witch of Bixler Gap.

All that is only conjecture, of course, since too much time has passed since the witch made this gap her home. Moreover, my further inquiries determined that locals know of no cemetery here with any Bixler tombstones, nor of any in a family plot that might confirm the names of those mentioned in the story. Similarly, no remnants of the original Bixler homestead are known of either. It's as though the Bixlers want that old witch tale to remain hidden in the dark hollows of Bixler Gap.

LOCATION:
The Blue Mountain parallels Route 322 along the border of Mifflin County and Juniata County.

DD GPS COORDINATES:
Bixler Gap: 40.5676, -77.5426

DRIVING DIRECTIONS:
Take the Port Royal exit off Route 322 and follow it through Port Royal to Old Port. Turn right onto Route 33 (Hawstone Road) and follow it through Shawnee and then pass Kangaroo Drive on the left. The next left is Rowles Road which dead ends back in Bixler Hollow.

CHAPTER 5

INDIAN STEPS—
REVISITED[22]

In my *Pennsylvania Mountain Landmarks Volume 1*, Chapter 2, titled "Stairways to the Stars," I discuss the unusual stone steps on the southern face of Tussey Mountain in Henry's Valley of Huntingdon County, known locally as The Indian Steps. It is a series of stone steps whose origins have been a source of speculation and debate for generations. However, since writing that chapter, new evidence has come to light that may help clear up that mystery, and in this chapter, we will discuss that possibility.

After making the strenuous climb up the Indian Steps, the determined hiker will reach the famous Mid State Trail, which crosses the mountaintop and stands as a lasting monument to Tom Thwaites, its progenitor and proponent. The steps end there, but the Indian Steps Trail continues down the northern face of the mountain toward the Centre County villages of Rock Springs and Pine Grove Mills.

The stone stairway itself has been the subject of conjecture and mystery for decades, and to this day there is debate as to who might have built them and why. Neither J. Simpson Africa in his *History of Huntingdon and Blair Counties*, nor John Blair Linn in his *History of Centre and Clinton Counties* mention the Indian Steps, and so it was left to Henry W. Shoemaker, that

---

22. Much useful information on Henry Shoemaker's approach to the legend of the Indian Steps was taken from Simon Bronner's fascinating biography of Shoemaker, *Popularizing Pennsylvania*.

Indian Steps trailhead and sign. (Harry's Valley, Huntingdon County)

prolific collector of Central Pennsylvania legends and folktales, to record its story for posterity.

Shoemaker, however, has been discredited for his propensity for embellishing, and even inventing, many of the tales he preserved in his multiple volumes and articles on such accounts, and in this essay, we'll critique his claims about the Indian Steps and try to establish our own theory as to its origins.

The stone stairway on Tussey Mountain is not unique in Pennsylvania, nor in the world for that matter. In the British Isles, for example, there is one flight of stone stairs that has captured the imagination of the inhabitants of that land of romance and legend for centuries. Located near Beetham in Cumbria, England, the narrow passageway is referred to as the Fairy Steps by locals.

These rectangular stone steps are so symmetrical and well-placed that they appear not to have been randomly fashioned by the forces of nature. Leading up through a narrow crevice formed by two gigantic rock ledges, the steps are so small and the corridor so narrow that humans find it impossible to walk up or down the passageway without touching its stone walls.

Hence the belief that the steps were placed there by fairies, and that if you make a wish at the top of the stairs and manage to walk down and not touch the walls, the fairies will grant your wish. I've chosen this stairway to serve as a nice segue into some mysterious stone stairways that can be found in the mountains of Pennsylvania.

I've never found any stone stairways on Pennsylvania mountainsides that are said to be the product of elfin hands, nor have I discovered any that are thought to be haunted in some way, but there are impressive flights of isolated stone steps on different Pennsylvania mountain slopes that may present the occasional hiker who comes upon them unexpectedly for the first time with as much of a mystery as the Fairy Steps do to hikers initially encountering those odd stone steps in England.

To these Pennsylvania hikers the questions must naturally arise as to who built these flights of fancy—that appear to be nothing more than that—and why did they do so in such out-of-the-way places. However, a little research usually confirms the reasons as to why they are there and who built them, and there are several notable examples that can be cited to illustrate this point.

Of course, one of the most well-known of these landmarks is the famous Thousand Steps in Huntingdon County; but Showers Steps in Berks County, and Fox's Path in Perry and Cumberland Counties are other notable examples as well.

The Thousand Steps Trail is a section of the rugged Standing Stone Trail which passes through Jacks Narrows—a wild defile that itself is steeped in history and legendary lore and which passes between the local communities of Mount Union and Mapleton Depot.

The Trail takes its name from the many stone steps found here that extend up the mountainside, and which it is said, actually number one thousand and forty-three. Their presence in such a remote spot may seem quite mysterious, but a large historical marker here sheds some light on that mystery.

The sign explains that on the mountaintop at one time there was a large quarry where employees of the Harbison-Walker firebrick company

A view of the Indian Steps ascending Tussey Mountain

quarried the vast deposits of ganister rock, or Tuscarora sandstone, found here. Initially a dinky train was used to transport the rocks to the firebrick refractories below, and workers could ride them up to the quarries. However, when trucks began to replace the trains, workers had to make a steep climb up the mountain to get to their place of work. Then, during an idle work period in 1936, the company had their men build the steps up the mountain to make their daily climbs easier.

Those are the steps that remain here yet today, and the pathway is considered by many to be one of the most popular hiking trails in that area. And the rewards, for those reaching the summit, are some of the finest panoramic views in the state. Vistas of Jacks Narrows, glimpses of Huntingdon, Mapleton, and Mount Union, and cascading mountain ranges fading off in the distance, make the climb worthwhile.

Similarly, Showers Steps, on the Blue Mountain above the small town of Bethel in Berks County, has a well-known provenance. Built in the 1930s by the Showers brothers in their desire to have an access trail to the Appalachian Trail on the mountaintop, this stone stairway provides a good aerobic workout for those who make the ascent to enjoy the panoramic view from the heights at the peak.

Then there is a stone-bordered pathway on the Blue Mountains near a scenic mountain pass called Sterretts Gap that connects the counties of Perry and Cumberland. Residents of the nearby villages of Dromgold and Sherman's Dale refer to it as Fox's Path, thereby preserving the memory of the man who built it.

It is not a staircase, but a dirt path demarcated on both sides its entire length by high stone walls that consist of loose boulders piled on top of one another. The pathway begins in Perry County near Fox's Hollow, a remote mountain glen named after the first settler here. He was a farmer or trapper who made frequent trips to Carlisle in Cumberland County, and who blazed this shortcut over the mountain. It was a rocky path, and in order to make it an easier trek, he threw the rocks on it to the sides until he had a smoother rock-free trip.

It can be seen, then, that the provenance of several seemingly out-of-place stone stairways found in the Pennsylvania mountains can still be found if the right sources are consulted (I'm indebted to locals in Berks and Perry Counties I interviewed in 1980 and in 2001 for the information on Showers Steps and Fox's Path). However, that still leaves us with that quite remarkable span of stone steps on Tussey Mountain of Centre and Huntingdon County whose origins are still cloaked in mystery.

The Indian Steps, as they are called, seem to reveal their origin in the name assigned to them. It is notable that many early folklorists, including Henry W. Shoemaker, promoted the idea that this manmade staircase was built by Indians for military purposes. However, any research into the way Indians waged war will easily prove this theory to be nothing more than myth; a delightful story that adds to the romance of the mountains.

In the first place, that meticulous historian Paul A. W. Wallace in his *Indian Paths of Pennsylvania* makes no mention of any such Indian path over Tussey Mountain and down to Rock Springs. Furthermore, the Indian origins of the steps was not supported by the gentlemen I like to call (and who said he would not object to my doing so) "the grandfather of the Mid State Trail." In my conversations with Tom Thwaite, planner and developer of that highly popular hiking trail that spans across the state, I asked him about the famous steps and who built them.

He agreed that it was not Native Americans, and postulated that the best explanation for their existence seems to be that the landholder of that section of mountain timberland felt he needed to create a prominent boundary line between his land and that of a local iron company's adjacent land. Driven by a fear that, in their insatiable need for wood to fuel their iron furnaces, the ironmasters would indiscriminately cut down his timber, he built the steps in what must have been a back-breaking and seemingly endless task.

Then, of course, there is Henry Shoemaker's take on the matter. Although his stories are considered apocryphal by many, they are nonetheless entertaining and enjoyable, and it has proven just as enjoyable to me to try to discover Shoemaker's inspirations behind them. In this essay we will look at one of his most famous tales; one recorded in the chapter titled "The Indian Steps," in his volume of the same name.

Published by Shoemaker in 1912, this was the third volume in a twelve-volume set, which he averred, in the introduction to his twelfth volume titled *More Allegheny Episodes*, "should be labelled, *Pennsylvania Folklore Series Vols. I, II, II, IV*, and so on, to properly identify them as scientific productions." In that same introduction he also confessed that "it might look as if the kernel of our stories has been too deeply imbedded in the local color and descriptions which have been woven about the narratives."

He then revealed more of what he defined as "the great glaring error of the series" by noting "If the stories had been printed word for word, in the

Another view of the Indian Steps ascending Tussey Mountain

language of the Pennsylvania mountain people who told them to him, then it would be exact, personal, definitive folklore."

In my opinion there is an even greater "glaring error" in many of Shoemaker's stories, and that is his disregard for, or distortion of, historical facts. It takes little effort to find out just how "footloose and fancy free" he was with those facts when writing his tales, and his *Indian Steps* is no exception.

For those who have never read the story, a brief summary is in order. Shoemaker, in his introduction to *Volume III*, states "The Indian Steps from which this present volume receives its name is an interesting land-mark in the Tussey Mountains, not far from Pennsylvania Furnace, in Centre County. The Steps were made, so tradition states, to enable Indian warriors from the southern part of the State to quickly cross the mountains when they invaded their northern rivals. In this vicinity was enacted, about the year 1600, one of the bloodiest battles recorded in the annals of the Redmen. It only lasted for a day, but it ended by the southern Indians being driven out of the Spruce Creek Valley and across the mountains, their warriors being nearly annihilated."

In the highly romanticized and grossly exaggerated Indian Steps story that follows in the first chapter of the book, Shoemaker tells of an athletic contest between the two tribes, with precise counts of victories scored in each event and the exact number of animals served to the hungry warriors following the contest. Then, typical of many of Shoemaker's tales that often include love stories about a man and a maid, he expands the Indian Steps tale to tell of a thwarted love match between a chieftain of the southern tribe and the beautiful "Princess Meadowsweet" in the northern band.

The defeat at the athletic contest and anger over the refusal of the north-ern chieftain to countenance the love affair in question supposedly then led the southern Indians to decide to wage war against their northern rivals. As part of their war plan, says Shoemaker, the southern or "Kishacoquillas Indians" proceeded to build a flight of stone steps up the Stone Valley side of Tussey Mountain. According to Shoemaker, the Indians reasoned that by doing so they could ascend the mountain more rapidly and thus make a "flying attack" upon their enemies, thus increasing their chance of victory, and once having achieved that victory, would "finish the steps down the northern slope of the mountain."

Given Shoemaker's penchant for inventing and exaggerating his stories, it is most probably the case that his "Indian Steps" is just one more typical example of his literary license. Indeed, it's safe to say that his rendition is nothing more than a good story that adds a romantic touch to this partic-ular area. So, let's begin by looking at this story from three perspectives. First, a geographical one as far as where Indian trail pathways were actually located in Pennsylvania. Then, a look at the Native American strategies during war, and finally, the locations of actual iron furnaces that were once in operation near the Indian Steps.

The definitive source for information on the Indian trails of Pennsylvania can be found in that minutely-detailed volume titled *Indian Paths of Pennsylvania*. Written by the highly-respected and trustworthy scholar Paul A. W. Wallace, this work contains descriptions of the many Indian trails that once crisscrossed the state, along with detailed maps of where they were located in relation to present-day towns and roadways. Out of all those maps and descriptions there are only two paths that show the areas in which we are interested.

The first is the Kishacoquillas Path (page 78), which was used by the Kishacoquillas Indians, whose village was located at present-day Lewistown, Mifflin County. This path led over the Seven Mountains and into the present-day town of Milesburg, Centre County, where the infamous chief Bald Eagle's village was located. This is the only northerly path described in the book that shows a trail over the mountains from the Kishacoquillas' village in the south.

The second path in Wallace's book that is of interest is one he calls the Penns Creek Path (page 126), which ran from Sunbury, Northumberland County, to Frankstown, Blair County. On the map of that path Wallace shows the village of Rock Spring in Centre County. However, he does not show any path whatsoever which heads from that small town and goes up and over Tussey Mountain to the south. This fact in itself casts strong suspicions about Shoemaker's "historical facts," doubts which are further strengthened when other historical sources are consulted.

One of the most trusted sources for information on the history of the Lenni Lenape, and other tribes of the mid-Atlantic region, is a treatise on that subject written by Reverend John Heckewelder. He was a Moravian missionary based in Ohio and Bethlehem, Pennsylvania, who preserved a record of his experiences with and impressions of the Native American tribes of these areas with whom he interacted during the eighteenth century.

Published by the Historical Society of Pennsylvania in 1818, it has been republished many times and includes invaluable details regarding the history of those tribes, their relations with other tribes and settlers, as well as their spiritual beliefs, government and politics, education, language, social institutions, dress, food, and other customs. It is in this volume that we find some accounts that are particularly germane regarding the Indian Steps.

On page 106 of Heckewelder's *History, Manners, and Customs of the Indian Nations*, for example, he notes that "In their wars they are indifferent about the means which they pursue for the annoyance and destruction of their adversaries, and that surprise and stratagem are as often as employed by them as open force."

Then on page 177 he goes on to say "Courage, art, and circumspection are the essential and indispensable qualifications of an Indian warrior. When war is once begun, each one strives to excel in displaying them by stealing upon his enemy unawares, and deceiving and surprising him in various ways. On drawing near to an enemy's country, they endeavor as much as possible to conceal their tracks; sometimes they scatter themselves, marching at proper distances from each other for a whole day, and more, meeting, however, again at night, when they keep a watch; at other times they march in what is called *Indian file*, one man behind the other, treading carefully in each other's steps, so that their numbers may not be ascertained by the prints of their feet.

"The nearer they suppose themselves to be to the enemy, the more attentive they are to choosing hard, stony, and rocky ground on which human footsteps leave no impression; soft, marshy and grassy soils are particularly avoided, as in the former the prints of the feet would be easily discovered, and in the latter the appearance of the grass having been trodden upon might lead to detection; for if the grass or weeds are only bent and have the least mark of having been walked upon, it will be almost certainly perceived, in which the sharpness and quickness of the Indians' sight is truly remarkable!"

Given Heckewelder's impressions, it would seem that there is little likelihood that Shoemaker's southern Indians would have gone to the trouble of building the Indian Steps in hopes of using them to surprise their enemy to the north in a lightning attack. The effort required to build the steps would have resulted in a flurry of activity, which certainly would have been noticed by hunters and scouts of the enemy tribe. We can safely conclude then, I propose, that building stone steps up one side of a mountain to use in a surprise attack on an enemy tribe right on the other side of the same mountain would not have been a strategy employed by Indians.

The final nail in the coffin for the idea that Indians constructed the so-called Indian Steps on Tussey Mountain can be found in a book written by Penn State folklorist Simon J. Bronner titled "Popularizing Pennsylvania—Henry W. Shoemaker and the Progressive Uses of Folklore and History." In this interesting and comprehensive biographical study of Henry Shoemaker and the reasons he may have written his stories the way he did, Bronner addresses Shoemaker's Indian Steps.

Here Bronner categorically states (see pages 114-115) that John H. Chatham, one of Shoemaker's most prolific sources for his folktales and legends, and a former schoolteacher, "was responsible for the legend of the Indian Steps." Apparently, Chatham wrote a letter to Shoemaker on January 12, 1911, in which he expressed his appreciation of Shoemaker's "Legend of Penns Cave" and suggested that Shoemaker could develop a similar tale based on Chatham's memory of an interesting landmark near one of his former country schoolhouses, located near Baileyville in Centre County. "I think a plot could be designed for another good Indian story at the Indian Steps," Chatham wrote.

"He located the tale," says Bronner, "just on the line of Centre and Huntingdon County at the head of Spruce Creek, thirteen miles west of Boalsburg and fifteen miles west of State College." Then, in that same letter, Chatham proceeded to summarize his idea for the story [sic].

"Here for some reason the Indians did work, they built a stone road over the Tussey rut. Consisting of a series of stone steps from the top to the bottom of the Mountain, and the same passage is used by the present inhabitants in crossing the range to Stone Valley—I think we could get up an Indian war between the Susquehannox and the Kishacoquillas Indians and have the battleground on the Barrens about two miles from the steps. Then we could people the upper waters of the Susquehanna and Bald Eagle Creek and the vast region between the creek and river to Sumamohining, with the Susquehannox and the Juniata Valley and all that region to the Bald Eagle Mts with the Kishacoquillas Indians, and there would be ample room for them to fight on the glades and barrens of Spruce Creek."

The idea obviously struck a chord with Shoemaker, who without a doubt, picked up Chatham's idea, added romantic details, created fictional characters to fill out the story, then claimed "that it was told to him by the old folks."

It seems from Chatham's letter in 1911 that the idea that Indians built the Indian Steps was apparently a prominent belief when he taught school near the steps years before. It was a belief that has continued down to the present day, but to those who knew more about the area and its history, it was not an idea that they could espouse.

As noted, this notion was certainly not supported by Tom Thwaites, who instead felt strongly that the landholder of this section of mountain timberland, driven by a fear that in their insatiable need for wood to fuel their nearby iron furnaces, the ironmasters would indiscriminately cut down his timber, built the steps in what must have been a back-breaking and seemingly endless task. Thwaites' theory has merit, considering the iron furnaces that were once located near here, and which no doubt gave the local landowner good reason to worry.

Geographically, the Indian Steps on Tussey Mountain are located, as the crow flies, about midway between Pennsylvania Furnace, Centre County, several miles to the northwest, and Greenwood Furnace, several miles to the southeast. Both of those locations were once the sites of, and named from, large and thriving iron furnaces: Pennsylvania Furnace (in operation from 1813 to 1888) and Paradise Furnace (operated from 1834 to 1904). Likewise, about one mile southeast of the road (Harry's Valley Road) leading back to the Indian Steps Trail, along present-day Route 26, was once a smaller iron furnace named Monroe Furnace (in operation from 1846 to 1863).

All three of these working furnaces would have needed to harvest timber off the surrounding ridges to keep their furnaces burning. And at the same time, during the last decades of iron furnace operations, lumbering companies were harvesting timber off of those same ridges. Therefore, it seems likely that the idea held by Tom Thwaites regarding the steps being constructed by the owner of a timber stand on Tussey Mountain to demarcate his land from that of lumbering or iron furnace companies seems increasingly reasonable.

However, there is one last possibility that makes sense as well. In an article titled "The Indian Steps" published in the *Centre Daily Times* of State College on March 4, 2019, author Chris Rosenblum sites mapmaker Michael Hermann as having interviewed a 97-year-old gentlemen about the Indian Steps in 1998.

According to that long-lived gentleman, the Civilian Conservation Corps (CCC) in the 1930s sometimes constructed long rock stairways over former logging skidways in order to repair and use them for more logging operations. However, as this would have occurred many years after the time that John Chatham referred to the steps in 1911, the CCC cannot be credited with building the Indian Steps.

That does not mean that logging or iron furnace companies did not build similar rock skidways during their lumbering operations here during the 1880s and 1890s. What is interesting as well is that the steps only exist on the southern slope. There are no steps on the northern slope.

In conclusion then, it seems in my opinion that the best explanation for the existence of the Indian Steps on Tussey Mountain is that they are there as a result of timber harvesting operations of the late nineteenth and earlier twentieth centuries. Despite the name and the legend, they are not of Native American origin. However, that name and the legend will no doubt survive as a quaint reminder of Pennsylvania's storied past, and in doing so they might help to preserve this part of the state's natural beauty and its legendary lore, which no doubt will continue to provide the same sense of mystery and romance that have colored one of Pennsylvania's most impressive mountain landmarks over the years.

FOOTNOTE: This same article was originally published by the Centre County Historical Society in their Summer 2023 *Mansion Notes* publication (Volume 45, Number 3) with the title of "The Mystery of the Indian Steps."

LOCATION: The entrance point to the **Indian Steps Trail** begins on the southern face of Tussey Mountain in Henry's Valley of Huntingdon County.

DD GPS COORDINATES:
40.7033971°N, -77.9344467°W

DRIVING DIRECTIONS:
Follow Route 45 West out of Boalsburg and continue to Pine Grove Mills. At the traffic light in Pine Grove Mills bear left onto Route 26 South toward McAlevy's Fort and to Jo Hayes Vista at the mountain top. From there continue down the south side of the mountain until you see the first road on the right. This is Harry's Valley Road. Turn right onto Harry's Valley Road (road sign is not easily seen), and within five miles you'll see the trail sign for Indian Steps Trail on the right. This is the trail that will take you onto the Indian Steps and up to the Mid-State Trail on the mountain top. It is a steep, rocky trail, so dress accordingly.

CHAPTER 6

THE BLOODY ROCK

For those who are not familiar with the frontier history of Pennsylvania, I think that this chapter should begin with some mention of the 1778 events that occurred in the Wyoming Valley of Luzerne County, which emboldened the Indians to attack settlements here and all along the Pennsylvania frontier during that same year and during other years of the Revolutionary War. These bloody attacks created a widespread panic all across the frontier and caused many settlers to abandon their farms and homesteads; an evacuation later described by historians as "The Great Runaway."

It was because of the many bloody conflicts that occurred along the Pennsylvania frontier during both the French and Indian War of the 1750s and the Revolutionary War of the late 1770s that Pennsylvania was referred to by some historians as a "dark and bloody ground." However, even though other states suffered similar attacks and had their own dark and bloody grounds, Pennsylvania, as a middle colony, bore more than its share of Indian raids, and nowhere were they more intense than in the Wyoming Valley. Although historians have preserved accounts on most aspects of the Wyoming Valley events, the legendary record has something to say about the matter as well, and it is one such record that we want to explore in this chapter to see if it contains any facts that may have escaped the watchful eye of the historian.

Of all the Indian outrages and massacres that occurred in the Wyoming Valley between the years 1763 and 1781, the one that is most remembered

Memorial to and grave site of the victims of the July 1778 Wyoming Massacre. (Located in the borough of Wyoming, Wyoming County)

is the massacre of Colonel Zebulon Butler's forces on July 3, 1778. The prelude to this terrible event began on July 2 when a force of four hundred British soldiers and Tories (Americans who were British sympathizers), along with seven hundred Seneca warriors, attacked and captured Forts Wintermoot and Jenkins, at or near present-day West Pittston.

Several other small forts, all within limits of present-day Wilkes-Barre, capitulated on the same day because of the lack of cannons inside the forts and the lack of able-bodied defenders (most of the valley's men were off fighting with the Continental Army.) However, the events of July 2 were merely a preview of the horrible defeat that was to follow the next day.

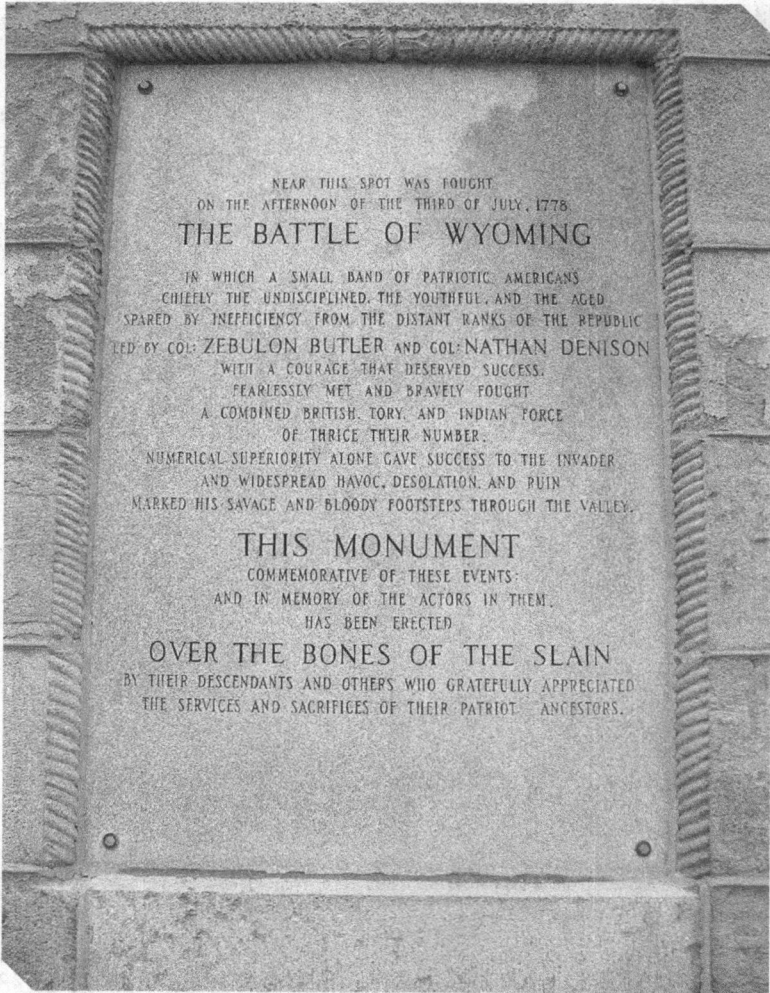

Plaque on the Memorial dedicated to a "small band of patriotic Americans that fearlessly met and bravely fought a combinded British Tory and Indian force of thrice their number."

Colonel Zebulon Butler, on leave from his duties in the Continental army and aware of the events of the previous day, took charge of the settlers who were left on July 3. The forces he had left to protect them hardly seemed adequate since his recruits, mostly old men and young boys, were unseasoned and untrained troops. Consequently, an objective observer would without doubt have not given them a ghost of a chance of defeating the enemy that was on their very doorstep.

Nonetheless, on July 3, Colonel Butler rallied his forces at the stockade whose name was derived from the first settlers who built it. They were Connecticut men, and there were forty of them. So, it was at Forty Fort that Butler took his stand. The seasoned Colonial thought he could hold the old bastion until reinforcements arrived, but more petulant personalities prevailed, including that of hot-headed Lazarus Stewart, leader of the infamous Paxton Boys who had murdered innocent Conestoga Indians sheltered in the Lancaster County jail in 1763.

Caving in to the urgings of his troops, Colonel Butler allowed them to leave the fort to attack the enemy, but before letting them go on their sortie he reminded them of the danger they were facing.

"Men," said Butler in grave tones, "yonder is the enemy. The fate of the Hardings tells us what we have to expect if defeated!"[23]

The reference to the Hardings was an appropriate one, not only because of its effect of impressing upon the men the danger they were about to face, but also because it touches upon the legendary realm of the story, which we will explore in more detail later. Suffice it to say for now that Butler's warning was ignored by the outnumbered patriots, and of the four hundred who left the fort to do battle, only sixty survived.

The others, including the impetuous Stewart, were either shot down like dogs during the fight, or cruelly tortured to death once captured. Subsequent accounts lamented that so many local militiamen were slaughtered, and the valley left in such a sorrowful state, that those forts that remained were "filled with widows and orphans."[24]

As details of the terrible massacre reached settlers along the north and west branches of the Susquehanna, a general panic quickly became widespread, and many took flight. Soon, except for the towns of Sunbury and Northumberland, there were no northern outposts left to stand against the rising tide of Tories and Indians, and even in those two places only the bravest of the brave stayed behind. It appears everyone else was thoroughly intimidated by the emboldened Indians, who now swept down upon larger groups of settlers than they had ever attacked in the past. However, if that reality, and the news of the fall of Forty Fort, were not enough to turn even the bravest men into more cautious ones, the mere details of what

23. C. Hale Sipe, *The Indian Wars of Pennsylvania*, 550.
24. Sherman Day, *Historical Collections of the State of Pennsylvania*, 439.

happened at Forty Fort, and the fate of the Wyoming Valley survivors after the Forty Fort defeat, would have been the turning point for many.

Names of the Seneca chiefs who led the attack against Forty Fort were no doubt included in the accounts of the battle that reached the frontier. The chiefs' names would have been familiar to many, not only because these warriors had such fierce reputations as hardened foes of the white encroachers but also because they were known for their ferocity when in battle. And so it was that the names of Red Jacket, Big Tree (*Ga-Oun-Do-Wah-Nah*) and "He-who-goes-in-the-smoke" (*Gi-En-Gwah-Toh*) became intertwined with the history of the valley.[25]

Accounts of that terrible time in Luzerne County form a historical record that for us today lends credence to the old adage that truth is stranger than fiction. On the other hand, it's also been said that the annals of the Wyoming Valley's original families "form a romance of themselves," but this in turn means, in the opinion of one prominent historian, that "folklore has been hard at work on the Battle of Wyoming," producing "a number of distortions that need to be corrected."[26]

Exaggerations and distortions about the battle, that were no doubt included in the graphic details of the battle's aftermath, eventually created a high level of consternation and fear along the upper stretches of the Susquehanna. And included in those lurid accounts would have been seemingly unbelievable but totally accurate descriptions of how, that night, the blaze of burning buildings lit up the entire valley, as terrified survivors, some who had been scalped alive, fled to the relative safety of the Pocono Mountains beyond Stroudsburg to the north.

In addition, the graphic narrations about the confusion, devastation, and bloodshed would have also undoubtedly included an account of all the people who had survived the brandished tomahawk and scalping knife only to meet death in the terrible wilderness they had to pass through on their way to what they thought would be a place of refuge. And these were the spots, these wilderness dying places where the most fatalities occurred due to exposure, starvation, and the like, that were later referred to as the "Shades of Death."[27]

---

25. C. Hale Sipe, *The Indian Wars of Pennsylvania*, 556; Sherman Day, *Historical Collections of Pennsylvania*, 438.

26. Paul A. W. Wallace, *Indians in Pennsylvania*, 161–162.

27. C. Hale Sipe, *The Indian Chiefs of Pennsylvania*, 488–489.

The Bloody Rock. Still marked with its red discoloration patch—safely protected under a secure steel grate.

As terrible and frightening as the descriptions of the attack on Forty Fort, and the narrations about the Shades of Death might have been, they probably paled in comparison to the scenes of horror that were brought to mind when people heard about the events that occurred after the battle at another place in the valley; a place that would become known to history as The Bloody Rock. And it was no doubt the accounts of the activities that took place here that left many settlers along the West Branch "doubtful," in the words of militia Colonel Samuel Hunter, "whether tomorrow's sun shall rise on them freemen, captives, or in eternity."[28]

28. Carl Carmer, *The Susquehanna*, 135.

The rock is still there, heavily enclosed under steel grating to prevent those self-entitled despoilers who call themselves artists from spray painting it with their gaudy designs. There is, however, a slight natural red discoloration on the rock that has led to its name; a title which seems appropriate given what is supposed to have happened upon it. There is some doubt about the accuracy of the accounts that tell of those events, and so it is perhaps at this boulder where folklore has been hardest at work and has created a few apparent distortions.

Historians disagree about who actually committed the atrocities that took place at the infamous rock. Although there seems to be consensus that an Indian woman was the bloodthirsty fiend who performed the dastardly acts, there is some confusion about who she was and what whipped her into a killing frenzy, and that's where history ends, and valley legends pick up the thread.

Historical accounts agree that the gallant defenders of Forty Fort were "slaughtered without mercy" and that those who lived to surrender were "subjected to the most cruel torture."[29] Those same accounts also agree that the cruelest and most gruesome episode of the many that occurred that fateful day was when sixteen of the staunchest captives were arranged in a circle around a large rock, the same one which is there yet today, rising to a height of about eighteen inches off the ground.

After the men were forced to kneel and place their heads upon the boulder, a hysterical Indian woman, identified by some as the Munsee woman known to the whites as Esther Montour, began to dance wildly around the stone. The frenzied performance was probably remarkable for a number of reasons, including the dancer's unearthly screams and the large tomahawk she waved around in the air over her head.

However, the ghastliest memory left on the minds of those who saw the "dance" was the part where the Indian woman, undoubtedly with a look of fury and hatred frozen upon her face, stopped now and then, as though she were playing some macabre game of Russian Roulette, to dash out the brains of a captive kneeling before her.

Although tradition has perpetuated the idea that the "priestess" who committed the many murders at the rock was Esther Montour, historians

---

29. C. Hale Sipe, *The Indian Wars of Pennsylvania*, 550.

do differ on the matter. There are those, on the one hand, that point out the kinder nature of Esther's mother and grandmother and conclude that Esther's inherited personality traits would be that of a gentle woman, rather than the she-devil who became known as the "fiend of Wyoming." On the other hand, other historians indicate that Esther may not have even been in the Wyoming Valley at the time at all, and also point out how, at the start of the Revolutionary War, she treated the Strope family, her prisoners at the time, "with great kindness."[30]

However, George Peck in his 1858 history of Wyoming County believed otherwise, stating "we see no good reason for doubting the part attributed to Catherine Montour, or Queen Esther, in the affair of the Bloody Rock."[31] It can be noted, though, that Peck may have confused Esther Montour with her sister, "French" Catherine Montour, who also had reason to harbor an intense hatred of the white race.

After all, it was Catherine's town, along Seneca Lake in present-day Schuyler County of New York State, that was singled out by General John Sullivan as the first Indian town to be destroyed on his punitive expedition into the Iroquois lake country; but that occurred a year later—in the summer of 1779. Therefore, Peck offers a reason why it was most likely Queen Esther who became a killing machine that day around the Bloody Rock.

"It was a right," notes Peck, "if not, indeed, the duty of the old queen to take sweet vengeance upon the prisoners which had fallen into her hands for the loss of her son who had been killed by a scouting party before the battle."[32]

Peck offers no further details about the death of Esther's son or the names of the scouts who may have killed him, but this is the place where valley legends pick up the story and offer some explanations of their own.

"One of the Hardings and his brother were partly responsible for the Wyoming Massacre," claimed one of Pittston's native sons, one day when he was telling us about the folktales and legends of the area.

"During the time of the Indian wars, the Indians were coming down along the Susquehanna River, and all the people went down and gathered

30. Paul A. W. Wallace, *Indians in Pennsylvania*, 172.
31. George Peck, *Wyoming, Its History, Stirring Incidents, and Romantic Adventures*, 290.
32. Ibid, 285.

in Forty Fort and waited for them," continued the man who had heard the old tales of Indian warfare while growing up in the area.

"Well, time went by and they didn't show up, and so the Harding brothers figured 'the hell with this,' and they went back up river to work their fields, since they had crops they needed to tend to. Then, while they were working in their fields, two Indians appeared on the scene and fired at the harvesters. The shots killed one of the Hardings, but the other fired at the Indians and killed one of them, who was just a young boy. Well, it turned out that this young boy was Queen Esther's son!

"That's why she went crazy after they took everyone prisoner at Forty Fort. She lined up all the settlers and she painted herself all up black and white, and one at a time she mashed their heads against the rock. Some broke and started running in all different directions, and a few made it to the river, escaped by swimming across, and told the story. I heard that as a kid!"[33]

Although the historical annals of the valley aren't quite that specific, they do note that on the 30th of June, Benjamin, Stuckley, and "young John" Harding, along with six other men, "went up the river from Wyoming into Exter to labor in their fields." Perhaps lulled into a false sense of security by the calm and balmy days of June, the men worked all morning and all afternoon without incident, but late in the afternoon they were attacked by a party of Indians who killed five of the nine, including two of the Hardings.

Three others were taken prisoner, but young John Harding managed to escape by diving into the Susquehanna at a place where several large willow trees were growing along the bank with their lithe branches hanging down over the water. The resourceful pioneer lad, hoping to avoid detection, concealed himself among the willow boughs while just keeping his mouth above water in order to breathe.

The Indians made a long and careful search for the escapee, and "at one time," Harding would later relate, "the Indians were so close they could have touched me." After his long submersion, the young pioneer did manage to escape, make his way back to the relative safety of the settlements, and tell them of the terrible fate of his brothers and the other men who had forfeited their lives in order to tend to their crops.[34]

33. Ken Davis (born 1937), interviewed March 2, 1972.
34. C. Hale Sipe, *The Indian Wars of Pennsylvania*, 549.

The following day, after John Harding had told them of the massacre, a small detachment of militiamen marched the eleven miles from Forty Fort to Exter in order to bury their fallen comrades. The appearance of the dead men must have been an unsettling sight, even to the hardened frontiersmen, for the dead bodies indicated that each man had given his last full measure before being killed.

All of the bodies had been scalped and mangled, but the faces and arms of Benjamin and Stuckley Harding had been "frightfully cut" and there were "several spear holes" through their torsos, indicating either the intensity with which they had fought for their lives or which were inflicted on their dead bodies by Indians that may have held a special grudge against them.[35]

These same historical accounts don't indicate whether the Hardings or any of their fellow victims killed any Indians during their struggle on the fields of Exter on what may have been an otherwise pleasant June afternoon in 1778. Therefore, it can't be said with any certainty that the Hardings killed Queen Esther's son that day.

However, on the following day, before the burial party began their gruesome task, two Indians who had concealed themselves in the woods beside the field and hoped to ambush any whites who came to take the bodies away, were, themselves, ambushed and killed by the burial detail.[36]

In an odd twist of fate, if local legendary accounts are to be trusted, one of those Indians turned out to be Gencho, the only son of Queen Esther. The men in the burial detail had no way of knowing who the two Indians they had killed might be, and so, in their rage and fury, the frontiersmen who shot Gencho made matters worse by also scalping him and mutilating his body with their tomahawks and knives.

It was this act of desecration, locals still believe, that most likely turned Queen Esther into the bloodthirsty fiend who dashed out the brains of thirteen helpless frontiersmen three days later around what was to become known to history as The Bloody Rock.[37]

---

35. Ibid.
36. Ibid.
37. Ibid.

The Wyoming massacre was the last straw for General George Washington. He had finally had it with the harassments of the Indians of the Six Nations; and exactly one year later, he ordered General John Sullivan to take five thousand seasoned troops into the heart of the Iroquois country and break the power of the great confederacy by destroying their villages.

So, in the summer of 1779, the "town destroyer," as the Iroquois would later call him, and his troops, marching out appropriately enough from Fort Wyoming, departed on their mission of devastation. It was a task that was completed with a thoroughness that was only to be seen again in wars of the modern era. At the end of their spectacular mission, Sullivan's army and its detachments, including General James Clinton's forces, destroyed almost fifty Indian towns in the Genesee Valley of New York State. Remarkably, despite the risks and many dangers, "only forty soldiers were lost by sickness and to the enemy."[38]

For the record, Fort Wyoming was a real place and was located "on the river common, about eight rods southwest of the junction of Northampton and River streets in the city of Wilkes-Barre" according to the panel of historians who were charged with investigating the matter.[39] Likewise, we also know that the incident at the nearby Bloody Rock, was, in the words of noted Wyoming Valley historian George Peck, "no mere fancy, but undoubted historical fact."[40]

Regardless of whether you believe the story or not, the rock is still there, and of all the valley's legends and folktales it is the story of the Bloody Rock, also referred to as "Queen Esther's Rock," that seems to be the tale that is most indelibly stamped upon the region. However, as some scholars have noted, it is at this spot where it might be said that folklore seems to have been hardest at work when turning its attention to the Battle of Wyoming.

Local imaginations were without doubt once stimulated by the fact that a portion of the infamous stone had a distinct reddish cast, enough so that it reminded more credulous onlookers of blood stains. Geologists say the red color is due to the ferrous content of this part of the rock, since iron tends to discolor in this way, but for generations the widespread belief

38. Ibid, 604, 741.
39. Thomas L. Montgomery, ed., *Frontier Forts of Pennsylvania—Volume I*, 427.
40. George Peck, *Wyoming, Its History, Stirring Incidents, and Romantic Adventures*, 284–285.

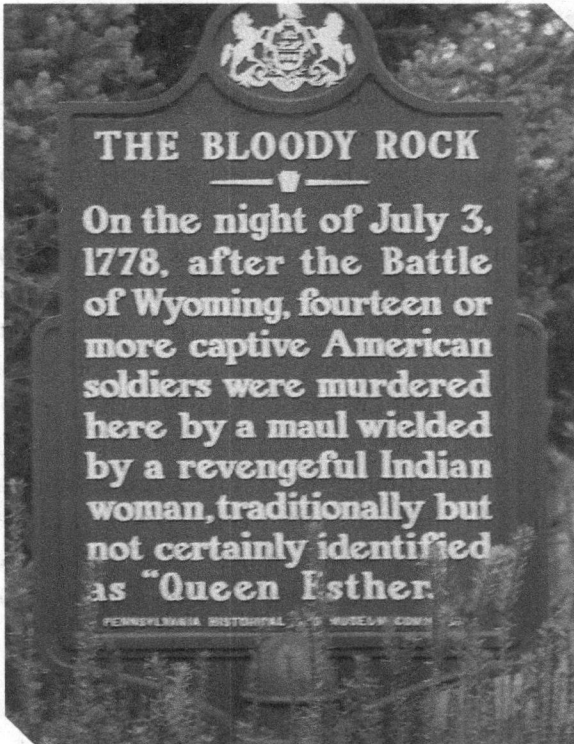

Historical marker at the Bloody Rock, which describes Queen Esther's revenge and her victims.

was that the red color was there because the blood of Queen Esther's many victims stained it this way.[41]

Today there are few of us who would believe that human blood would stain rocks in that way, and this disbelief is strengthened when it's considered that eradicable bloodstains on steps and floors are a fanciful feature of haunted manor houses and castles in the British Isles, with Smithills Hall in Lancashire and Moretham Tower in Yorkshire being among the most notable.

The "bloody footstep" at the stone threshold of one of the doors in Smithills Hall, is said to be a footprint from the boots of the lord of the manor, who had just tracked through the pool of blood of a young woman he had just stabbed to death for selfish reasons. It's said that the bloody

_____
41. Ibid.

footprint has endured to this day to serve as a condemnatory reminder of his foul deed.[42]

Similarly, indelible stains on the spiral stairs in Moretham Tower, the ancient seat of the Rokeby family, are said to be drops of blood from the knife of one of the medieval lords of the manor when he stabbed his beautiful wife to death in a fit of jealous rage and then beheaded her.[43]

The poor woman's skull is said to lie at the bottom of the Tees, a lake near the manor house, but it has never been found, unlike skulls of some of the victims of the Wyoming Massacre. Buried with all victims' bones in a common vault under the Wyoming Massacre Battle Monument in the town of Wyoming, the skulls are proof of the way these early settlers died.

The historical markers here indicate that some of the skulls have bullet holes where musket balls entered the cranium and snuffed out a life, and others show both bullet holes and the deep grooves of the scalping knife, morbid reminders which show how much those settlers were willing to sacrifice in order to gain the freedom and independence we often take for granted today.

LOCATION: This iconic artifact from Pennsylvania's storied part in the Revolutionary War, can be found on Susquehanna Street in the city of Wyoming, Luzerne County.

DD GPS COORDINATES:
41° 18' 29.6028" N, 75° 49' 54.0228" W

DRIVING DIRECTIONS:
Take US 11 into Wyoming. Turn east onto E. 8th St. Drive five blocks. At the traffic light, turn left onto Susquehanna Ave. Drive a half block. You'll see an insurance agency and brick building on the left. The rock is just across the street from these, on the right, just past a white two-story house.

42. John H. Ingram, *Haunted Homes and Family Traditions of Great Britain*, 563–567.
43. J. A. Brooks, *Britain's Haunted Heritage*, 162.

CHAPTER 7

WITCHES' HILL

On one of my many travels through Pennsylvania's farmlands and forests, I was brought to a screeching halt one day when exploring the backroads of Berks County. It was not an animal or another car that caused me to stop, but instead a puzzling road sign. Its unusual lettering had caught my attention, and I wanted to make sure I had read it correctly. On the sign were the words "Witchcraft Road" and they immediately fired my imagination. Mysterious. Intriguing. What interesting story led to that name?

The sweeping hilltop views of fields, red barns, stone farmhouses, and the towering peaks of the Blue Mountain in the distance added to the appeal and wonderment of this place, and so when I got home, I immediately began to find out all I could about what events led to the name of this road and whether there was a supernatural basis behind it.

Readers of the author's *Pennsylvania Fireside Tales* series are familiar with the many old-time witch tales preserved in those volumes, along with descriptions of the numerous superstitions and beliefs Pennsylvania mountain folk once held about the practice of witchcraft. As noted in these stories, it was surprising just how long their convictions lasted. It took a long time for them to be laid to rest, despite the advance of science and education, which indicated just how deeply entrenched they were.

Consequently, it's not surprising that some of these so-called witches, or *hexes* in the vernacular of the Pennsylvania Dutchman, became somewhat famous in the localities where they lived and where they performed their

Road sign at intersection of Haas Road and Witchcraft Road (Berks County)

View of Witchcraft Road and Witches Hill at the ridge top (Berks County)

View of the witches woods as seen from Witches Hill at the ridge top. (The woods are at the bottom of the hill on the left)

seemingly supernatural feats. Nonetheless, despite their reputations, most of their names have not come down to us, except for a few that have been recorded in historical records. Likewise, no monuments or historical markers have been erected to preserve a memory of their lives. That is why the road sign in Berks County is so unusual, and why it bears further explanation.

According to the older residents of the area who were consulted about the matter, their ancestors once considered the hilltop that Witchcraft Road ascends to be cursed by witches and demons (*Trottenkopfs* or Trotterheads in the vernacular of ancient southern Germany—it meant malevolent spirits.[44]) Their conviction was so strong, in fact, that they called the hilltop *Hexe Dans,* which some translate as Witches' Hill and others as Witches' Dance or Witches' Dance Hall.

The reason they thought this name was appropriate was because of the odd things that happened here. Strange lights were sometimes seen on the hilltop, and large areas of trampled crops that seemed to have no natural

44. Patrick Donmoyer, *Powwowing in Pennsylvania: Braucherei and the Ritual of Everyday Life,* 178.

In the witches woods. (Remnant of the woods as it looks today)

cause would appear in the hilltop's fields. Even more mysteriously, farmers noticed that when driving their herds of cattle along Witchcraft Road, the cows would occasionally stop and refuse to go any further, as though sensing an evil presence. Likewise, this same thing sometimes happened when they were riding their horses along the same road. Then there was that spot at the ridge top where no crops would grow at all.

The explanation for this infertile soil, they reasoned, was that malicious evil spirits were trysting with witches here. After all, wasn't there a great circular track on the hilltop, well-worn into the ground and made bare by the revelers' feet when dancing around and around during their devilish festivities? Moreover, the story claimed, when the witches tired of their prolonged hilltop trysts, they would slowly file their way back into a nearby deep ravine known as Witches' Hollow, where they resided. It was from beliefs such as this that Witches' Hill and Witchcraft Road came to be known as such, and also why the nearby mountain was eventually referred to as *Hexebarrich* or Hex Mountain.

Eventually, not to be outdone by the witches, locals decided to hold a ceremony of their own on Witches' Hill. Recalling a tradition from the Old Country, they decided that *Walpurgisnacht* was the perfect tradition to protect themselves from malicious hexes. Always conducted on the eve of the Saint Walpurga Christian feast day, typically on the night of April 30 and into the first day of May, it was a way to scare away all unwanted evils.[45]

It was also a way to herald the promise of springtime after the longer days of darkness and the freezing weather of winter they had just come through. Its rituals consisted of making noise, reciting prayers, and lighting bonfires to banish the forces of darkness and to open up entryways for the forces of light to illuminate their lives once again. Then local powwowers began to make use of the site as well, using it much like their counterparts in Northampton County were thought to use Hexenkopf Rock in that county (see the author's *Pennsylvania Mountain Landmarks Volume 3* and the chapter titled "Hexenkopf Rock" for details).

It was believed that good witches, also called *brauchers*, could remove spells that a black witch, or hex, had inflicted upon people or animals, by casting a counterspell that transferred the evil energy into a receptor such as a pile of rocks. Brauchers had done so for decades at the Witch's Head rock in Northampton County, which is what gave that place such a fearful reputation, and it was rumored that they also began to do so at Witches' Hill in Berks County. Knowing that it was a repository of evil energy, people were then not surprised when unexplainable things began to happen on Witches' Hill.

Strange events reportedly continue to this day, with cars stalling out next to a small patch of woods along the roadside. There are also those who report finding mushroom circles (*marrichel-ringe* to the Pennsylvania Dutchman) on the hilltop to this day. Once believed to be evidence of witches' dances, they are actually found in high places all along the Hex Road (Old Route 22 in Berks County). On the other hand, there are modern day recreations of the Walpurgisnacht bonfires that once were lit on Witches Hill to cleanse the area of evil spirits. Done only for nostalgic reasons today, the bonfires help recreate that aura that once was prevalent

---

45. J. Gordon Melton, *Religious Celebrations*, 915.

Road sign at intersection of Virginville Road and Witchcraft Road. (Two unique place names in Berks County, Virginville is situated along Maiden Creek. Both names derived from Ontelaunee, the Indian name for the creek, meaning virgin or maiden—see footnote # 7)

SCENE ALONG GEORGE'S CREEK
FAYETTE COUNTY, PA

Old postcard with title "Scene Along Georges Creek, Fayette County, PA." Moll Derry, the Witch of the Monongehela, lived in the woods that grew along this stream here and which gave the place its name. Thus, the name Witches Hill will always commemorate an era that science and education has otherwise eradicated.[46]

No witches' names have come down to us from the area of Witches Hill, but the historical record has preserved a few of the names of witches in other parts of the state, with the witch's degree of notoriety apparently being the reason for the survival of their names. Two of these deserve further mention, beginning with Margaret Mattson, the Witch of Ridley Creek in Delaware County, and Moll Derry, The Witch of the Monongahela in Fayette County.

Mattson and her Swedish husband Neels lived on a small farm between Crum and Ridley Creeks along the Delaware River in present-day Eddystone Township; the site is now an industrial park. Whether they had antagonized their neighbors or whether the accusations arose for reasons of jealousy is not known, but in 1683 Margaret was accused of bewitching farm animals and of being seen performing witchlike rituals beside large boiling cauldrons. The evidence was damning and so she was brought to trial.

No court system had yet been set up in William Penn's two-year-old colony, so her case was brought before the Pennsylvania Provincial Council on February 7, 1683. It must have invoked a lot of curiosity because the Philadelphia courtroom was packed. Not only were there members of a grand jury and a petit jury, the attorney general, and numerous witnesses, but William Penn himself attended the trial.

Witnesses came forth with a litany of supposed transgressions, and also claimed that they had often heard others say Margaret was a witch. Not being able to understand English, Mattson required an interpreter, but she must have had some degree of intelligence because she pleaded innocent to all charges. She also must have had some legal knowledge, since she is quoted as saying "witnesses speake only by hear say."

Her pleas did not fall on deaf ears. William Penn was certainly impressed, and after hearing her plea and considering the other testimonies, he asked her two final questions. "Art though a witch," which she denied. He then

---

46. Charles J. Adams, "Berks the Bizarre," *Reading Eagle*, February 11, 2015; based upon *Reading Eagle* columns written in 1925 by Robert Baker Bamford; and numerous online websites.

Historical sign erected beside the Hexebarger, or Witches' Hill, Somerset County. Woods where Prissy Rugg and her white stallion could once be seen, and where, some say, their ghosts still can be seen and heard!

asked her "Doth you fly through the air on a broomstick," to which she seemed to answer that she had, but perhaps only because she did not speak English and had not fully comprehended the translation.

Penn, with his great common sense, Quaker compassion, and deep skepticism of the witchcraft hysteria that was beginning to spread in the colonies, then declared that since there was no law in the province against flying around on a broomstick, Mrs. Mattson could not be charged for doing so. He went on to charge the jury, which after some deliberation, returned the following verdict: "Guilty of having the common fame of a witch, but not guilty in manner and form of which she stands indicted."

The punishment was nominal. The Mattsons were fined 50 pounds apiece, and Margaret was put on probation for six months. It was a remarkable example of Quaker restraint and common sense, given the fact that the infamous Salem Witch Trials occurred nine years later.[47]

---

47. Author Unknown, "Witches and Their Art in This County," *Chester Times*, April 15, 1902; http://laquaker.blogspot.com/2013/10/the-witch-of-redley-creek-only-quaker.html.

Moll Derry in Fayette County most likely would not have been as fortunate if tried by the Pennsylvania Provincial Council at the same time. Called the Witch of the Monongehela by locals who knew of her nefarious deeds, her reputation was widely circulated, but not much is known about her otherwise. It is thought that she was born about 1760, arriving here with her husband during the Revolutionary War. He was a Hessian mercenary who fought with the British initially, but the Derrys switched sides at some point, with Moll's husband becoming one of an elite group of colonial sharpshooters. He proved to be a standout, which was no small feat, as one of Daniel Morgan's famous riflemen. His unerring aim was admired by most of his comrades, but others claimed that it was too good to be true, and for it to be that good he had to be a "wizard," or it was because he rubbed himself with special magical potions prepared by his wife.

That was only one of many supernatural powers attributed to Moll. As her reputation grew, people from miles away would travel to her humble abode in the mountain mists and hollows of southwestern Pennsylvania

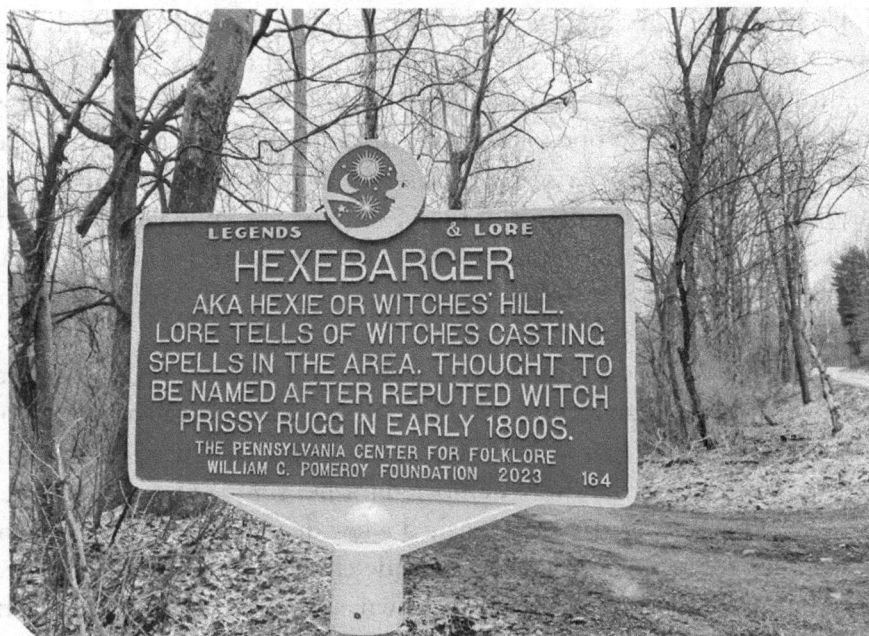

Close up of the Historical sign erected at the Hexebarger, or Witches' Hill, Somerset County. Note the interesting astrological images on the decorative emblem on the top of the sign.

because they believed not only that she could fly, but that she could also use her strange rituals to foretell their future, heal their ills, and protect them from misfortune. They also knew that she had helped many folks find missing cows, horses, and pocketbooks, and had even identified the thief in some cases. Although the stories of her miraculous deeds became favorite memories in the minds of Fayette Counties oldest citizens, they eventually were woven into the legendary fabric of the Monongahela Valley, told and retold as popular fireside tales.

However, as news of Moll's charitable deeds spread, there also came reports that she had acquired her uncanny abilities by making a pact with the devil. Such a covenant meant that anyone who crossed her would end up with cows who would not give milk, cream that would not turn to butter, and bread that would not rise. It was also said that she had supernatural control over rattlesnakes and had an army of them protecting her home. Moreover, it was believed that her retribution could turn deadly if she was really upset.

It was recalled, for example, that one day in 1794 three ruffians crossed Moll's path. They recognized her, and being the uncouth brigands they were, they mocked her and questioned her claims that she could foretell the future. The angry witch cursed them all and proclaimed they would all hang. Within a month one man, in a drunken rage, killed a tavern keeper and was hanged for his crime in Fayette County. The second man, after murdering a man in a bar fight in Ohio, suffered the same fate, also going to the gallows. The third man, hearing of the fate of his two companions, decided to hang himself rather than risk being executed in the same way by others.

Coincidence or not, it made a good story and enhanced Moll's reputation. On the other hand, those who knew her said that such an action on her part would have been out of character. She bore and successfully raised seven children and was most remembered for her simple lifestyle. As noted in an 1879 newspaper article, published a few decades after her death, she was remembered for her simple homemade clothes, and her love of coffee. And, the article continued, "As far as known, she harmed no one, and if she got her money and her coffee, she was always contented."[48]

---

48. Thomas White, *The Witch of the Monongahela: Folk Magic in Early Western Pennsylvania*; and numerous websites.

Although there were a few reputed witches whose life stories are preserved in history books and in newspaper accounts, there are seemingly none whose lives are commemorated by some sort of monument or historical marker. At least that was my opinion, until I found an exception to that rule in Somerset County. And what makes her story so interesting is that her base of operations was on a place also called the Hexebarger, or "Witches' Hill." Unlike the hill of that same name in Berks County, this one has an historical marker identifying its location, and on that marker is the name of the witch whose ghost, some say, still haunts Witches Hill, making the surrounding hills ring as she vowed she would do after she died.

For generations, residents of Turkeyfoot Valley in southwestern Somerset County have preserved the memory of their witch through oral history, but to preserve it for posterity, the Pennsylvania Center for Folklore in 2023 erected a permanent sign beside the hills through which she once enjoyed riding on her pure white horse.

The horse was a wedding present from her father after his daughter Priscilla, born in 1757, married Samuel Rugg and the newlyweds purchased a farm in Turkeyfoot Valley in 1789. The horse was to be used to help work their farm, but Prissy had other ideas. That's not surprising since she is remembered as being a nonconformist and not domestically inclined whatsoever. Her subsequent actions also seem to indicate that she may have become mentally unhinged at some point, as she was known to quit work early, unhitch her white horse, step onto a stump, and jump from it onto the horse. She would then ride it in circles around the stump, yelling to her husband that she would "make the welkin [sky] ring!"[49]

This unusual behavior got worse, as she then started to ride through town shouting curses and casting hexes upon people. Not surprisingly, the early German settlers who were her neighbors began to look upon her with suspicion and soon labeled her as a witch; began calling her the *Hex Berge*, or "Witch of the Hills." Their suspicions were flagrantly confirmed one day, when one of her evil spells apparently took effect upon a man who had maliciously killed her goose. The act enraged the old lady, and in her

---

49. Meredith Rogers, "A Pennsylvania Ghost Story," ESDCTA Magazine, November 2023; numerous websites; and the historic sign marking the site of the *Hexebarger*, which I found and photographed in 2025.

Another view of the woods at the Hexebarger, or Witches' Hill, Somerset County. Where Prissy Rugg once made "the welkin ring."

execrations and threats, she said she would cause him to walk like a goose for the rest of his life.

The very next day, the man, who was a coalminer, was injured in a mine accident that caused such damage to his legs that he could no longer bend them. Even after he finally regained the ability to walk, his legs remained so stiff that when he could walk, he actually looked like a walking goose!

Despite the fact that Prissy seemed to spend a lot of time administering to Revolutionary War soldiers when she made visits to their camps while riding through the hills on her white steed, her benevolences did little to assuage her neighbors' fear of her. Probably as a result of the curse she had successfully cast upon the man who killed her goose, those who saw her coming went scurrying for cover.

Like the maverick she was in life, her legacy did not pass on with her when she died in 1837. Her long shadow still invoked pangs of fear and waves of apprehension in valley residents for decades. Over time berry pickers on Hexie Hill, as they then referred to the hilltop and hills where

The old homestead standing today at the Witches' Hill, Somerset County. Could this have been the Rugg log cabin? It certainly adds a nostalgic link back to the time when Prissy Rugg lived in this same area.

she was once so fond of riding, claimed that they had seen a ghostly image of Prissy and her white horse gliding through the forest here. They even claimed, and some do yet today, that they could hear the hoofbeats of that horse, and also hear her screams and yells echoing through the hills. After all, they said, didn't she vow "to make the welkin ring" even after she died?[50]

ADDITIONAL REMARKS:

1. Genealogical records show that Priscilla Curtis Rugg, wife of Samuel Rugg, bore seven children to her husband.

2. Also referred to locally as the "Hexie", the exact boundaries of the *Hexebarger* or Witch's Hill in Somerset County cannot be placed exactly, nor can they be found on any map.

3. Prissy Rugg's gravesite can be found in the Rugg Cemetery, or Israel Rhoades Farm Graveyard, Lower Turkeyfoot Township, Somerset County.

50. Ibid.

4. Prissy Rugg was a distant neighbor to infamous Moll Derry. Prissy lived in Somerset County, while Moll lived directly to the east in adjacent Fayette County.

LOCATIONS:
Witches Hill, Berks County: Witchcraft Road is located in Berks County near Virginville.
Hexeberger, Somerset County: The historical marker for this site is at 1818 State Rte. 3007, near Confluence, PA.

DD GPS COORDINATES:
Witches Hill, Berks County: 40.8828829, -77.7870320
Hexeberger, Somerset County: 39.857361, -79.317767

DRIVING DIRECTIONS:
Witches Hill, Berks County: From Virginville, follow Route 143 northwest until you can turn left onto Virginville Road. Follow this road until you can bear right onto Witchcraft Road, which runs northwest towards Windsor Castle. At the highest point on the road is the area known locally as Witches' Hill, the place locals once believed was cursed by witches.

Hexebarger, Somerset County: From Confluence, follow Park Street through Ursina and onto Humbert Road. Continue on Humbert Road (State Route 3007) northward to the historical marker.

CHAPTER 8

HALF KING'S ROCKS

At the risk of presenting the reader with yet one more chapter on a Pennsylvania landmark that has strong connections to the Native Americans who were the original inhabitants of our state, I must do so once again, even though it may seem I'm dwelling too much on that subject. The reason I want to include this particular site is because I feel this place and the stories behind its unusual name deserve to be brought to the reader's attention. Moreover, that title itself has an interesting history, colored by legend, that requires some further elucidation.

In researching the legends, human interest stories, and historical basis for the stories I've preserved in my *Pennsylvania Fireside Tales* series and in this *Pennsylvania Mountain Landmarks* series, I was sometimes struck by how Native American chieftains were sometimes referred to as "kings" by the Europeans who dealt with them. It was a cognomen that seemed appropriate to the European colonists who dealt with the Aboriginals, but it was a misnomer to the natives, as far as their culture and the societal norms they practiced.

William Penn weighed in on the matter when he wrote of Native American politics. "Their government is by kings, which they call *sachema*... Every king hath his council, and that consists of all the Old and Wise men of the nation. Nothing of moment is undertaken, be it war, peace, selling of land, or traffick, without advising with them; and which is more, with the young men too. 'Tis admirable to consider, how Powerful the kings are, and yet how they move with the breath of their people."[51]

---

51. Albert Cook Myers, ed., *Narratives of Early Pennsylvania, West New Jersey, and Delaware 1630–1707*, 234–235; Richard S. and Mary M. Dunn, eds., *The Papers of William Penn, Volume 2*, 452–453.

In the Glen. (Forest and boulders in Jumonville Glen near the ambush site)

Colonel James Smith, leader of the famous Black Boys, so-called because of their blackened faces at the time of the incident, had his own opinion about the matter. In March of 1765, Smith and ten of his fellow frontiersmen bushwhacked a convoy of Indian traders transporting "war-like stores" to the warriors who they thought were raiding their frontier settlements.[52]

The traders had refused to relinquish their goods voluntarily, and so Smith and his men took matters into their own hands. Positioning his men in the trees along a mountain pass on Sideling Hill, near Greencastle in the Allegheny Mountains of Franklin County, the doughty Smith instructed his companions to use Indian tactics during their ambush. It proved to be the deciding factor, as the traders were forced to return empty-handed from whence they came.[53]

52. James Smith, *An Account of the Remarkable Occurrences in the Life and Travels of Colonel James Smith*, 108.
53. Ibid, 109–110.

Rock wall (on the left) in Jumonville Glen where Washington, the Half King, his Indian allies, and Washington's troops stood to ambush the French troops in the clearing below

The success of the battle against a regiment of the British Army guarding the pack train made Smith and his men famous. The so-called Allegheny Uprising went down in history since it was considered by many to be the first armed resistance to British authority at that time.[54]

James Smith knew the ways of the Indians well, having been captured by them at age eighteen in 1755, and then living with them until his release in 1760. During his captivity he became an accepted member of the village into which he was adopted. He learned as much about their ways as he could during his five-year captivity, keeping a daily journal of his experiences. It is from his years of living with them that he disputed the idea that the Indians had "kings."

"I have often heard of Indian kings," he would later write when composing his memoirs, "but never saw any." "How any term used by the Indians in their own tongue, for the chief man of a nation, could be rendered

54. Taken from the inscription on the Pennsylvania Historical and Museum Commission historical marker located near Mercersburg, Pennsylvania, titled "Black Boys Rebellion."

King, I know not. The chief of a nation is neither a supreme ruler, monarch, or potentate. He can neither make war or peace, leagues or treaties… nor can he refuse his assent to their conclusions, or in any manner control them. With them there is no such thing as hereditary succession, title of nobility, or royal blood, even talked of. The chief of a nation has to hunt for his living, as any other citizen. How then can they with any propriety, be called kings? I apprehend that the white people were formerly so fond of the name of kings, and ignorant of their power, that they concluded that the chief man of a nation must be a king."[55]

He was not far off the mark. Thinking that the hierarchical political structures were the same within Indian tribes and alliances as those in European countries, the European settlers in the New World presumed that the correct title for Native American leaders should be kings rather than chiefs. Although they probably did not grasp the full implications of the word, Native American tribes eventually accepted use of that appellation, perhaps for nothing more than assuring that both parties understood one another more clearly when engaged in treaty negotiations and land deals.

Regardless of the reason, the term eventually was applied to all chief spokesmen for any particular tribe. Thus we read of Wi-daagh as King of the Susquehanna Indians (see the author's chapter titled "Lochabar" in his *Pennsylvania Mountain Landmarks Volume 2* for some interesting details about this defamed sachem). Then there was a succession of Kings of the Delaware from 1712 through 1754, including *Shingas, Sassoonan, Netawatwees*, King Beaver, *Teedyuscung*, and perhaps others.[56] Out of all the sachem "kings" however, there was another chief who started out as a king but who eventually became known as the Half King. His story is a tragic one.

Tanacharison rose to prominence because of his skill as a peace negotiator. As such he handed over English captives at the end of the French and Indian War and helped negotiate a peaceful settlement to end Pontiac's War afterwards. Nonetheless, during the French and Indian War he found himself in a difficult situation. The Iroquois Confederacy tried to maintain a position of neutrality to ensure continuing trade with both the British

55. James Smith, *An Account of the Remarkable Occurrences in the Life and Travels of Colonel James Smith*, 147.

56. C. Hale Sipe, *The Indian Chiefs of Pennsylvania*, 88, 90, 100, 326–327.

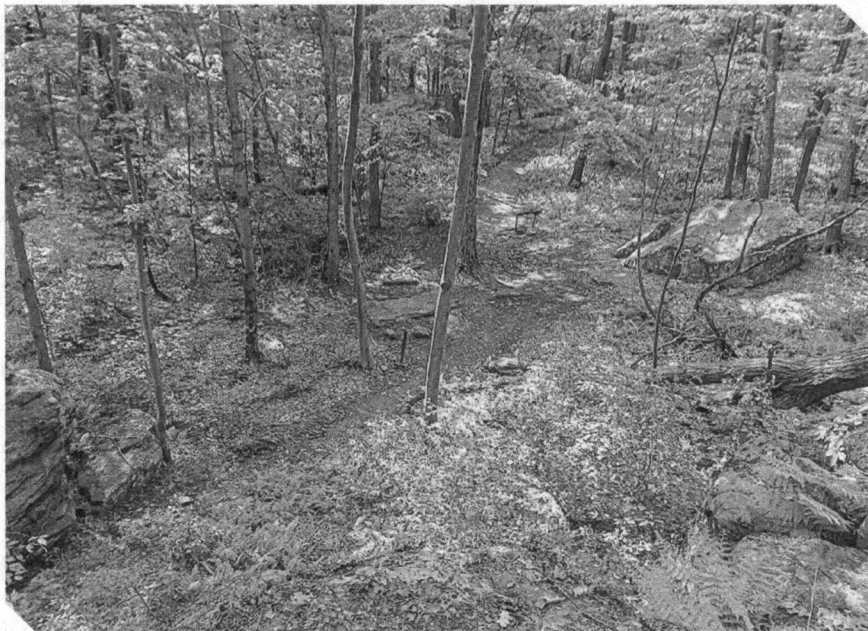

View of the French encampment site from atop the Rock wall in Jumonville Glen

and the French during that war, but Iroquois Confederation tribes chose one side or the other, depending upon which side was the most beneficial to their trade. *Tanacharison* sided with the British,[57] and we must implore the reader to bear with us as we share more history about that.

During the French and Indian War, he had joined a young George Washington to fight against the French. In the fall of 1753, Washington was carrying a letter from the governor of Virginia demanding that the French abandon their forts in what then was described as the Ohio Country. The territory was a loosely defined region between Lake Eire and the Ohio River and the center of a lucrative fur trade. It was claimed by both the French and the British. The French had solidified their claims to the area by building four forts within it: Presque Isle, Le Boeuf, Machault, and Duquesne. It was those forts that the Governor of Virginia wanted the French to abandon.[58]

---

57. Christine Calvo, "A Half-King in America," *American Historical Manuscript Collection (AHMC)*, New York Historical Society, March 23, 2016.
58. C. Hale Sipe, *The Indian Chiefs of Pennsylvania*, 146 ff.

On his way, Washington stopped at Logstown (present day Ambridge in Beaver County), then one of the largest and most politically significant Indian communities in western Pennsylvania.[59] Here he asked the presiding chief of the village for some warriors to accompany him and serve as guides. That chief was *Tanacharison*, the Seneca known as the Half King.[60] Stoked by his hatred of the French, the Half King, along with two other chiefs, agreed to join Washington. On November 30 they left Logstown, arriving at Fort LeBoeuf on December 11, 1753, in the middle of a raging snowstorm, only to be rebuffed by the French commander.[61]

Then in May of the following year, Tanacharison, still harboring ill feelings toward the French, was canvassing the forests of Chestnut Ridge, present-day Fayette County. Here he found "tracks of Frenchmen" and traced them to their encampment in an "obscure retreat" on the summit. He immediately sent a messenger to alert Washington, who was camped six miles away in the Great Meadows. Washington, fearing an attack upon his own forces, immediately set forth with forty or more of his troops.[62]

It was eight o'clock at night and raining heavily. Nonetheless, the well-trained force trudged through the heavy downpour, also fighting "a night of intense darkness and the obstacles presented by an almost impenetrable forest."[63] Hardly a situation for a rapid response to *Tanacharison*'s warning, which must have frustrated Washington, who would later write "We were frequently tumbled over one another, and often so lost that fifteen or twenty minutes' search would not find the path again."[64]

They finally found *Tanacharison* with a force of warriors about two miles north of the Chestnut Ridge summit. The parties agreed to join forces and attack the French, who they then tracked to an almost inaccessible rocky glen about a mile away. When they finally got close enough, the French were taken totally by surprise and made a mad rush for their weapons.

Firing commenced on both sides, but after fifteen minutes of fighting, the French were totally defeated with the loss of their entire force. Ten, including M. de Jumonville their commander, were killed, one was

59. George P. Donehoo, *Indian Villages and Place Names in Pennsylvania*, 92.
60. C. Hale Sipe, *The Indian Wars of Pennsylvania*, 154–158.
61. Washington Irving, "Logstown to Murdering Town," excerpted from his "Life of Washington."
62. C. Hale Sipe, *The Indian Wars of Pennsylvania*, 154–158.
63. Ibid.
64. Ibid.

Believed by some to be another depiction of Tanacharison, this public domain image is of a painting by artist Robert Griffing. However, he titled it "New Day, new rifle" without any reference to Tanacharison.

Artist's depiction of Tanacharison (artist Fred Threlfell) Found at
https://www.nps.gov/fone/learn/historyculture/people.htm

wounded, and twenty-one were taken prisoner. Only one of Washington's troops was killed. The inaccessible glen where the battle took place became known as the Jumonville Glen, thereby perpetuating the memory of the French commander who died there.[65]

Just as the opening shot at the battles of Lexington and Concord on April 19, 1775, was later described as "the shot heard around the world" because it sparked the American Revolutionary War, the opening shot at the Battle of Jumonville Glen could well be described as another "shot heard around the world." Described by some as the opening battle of the French and Indian War, it no doubt triggered that conflict, which began in earnest the following year.

SOME FURTHER NOTES:

Jumonville Glen is included on the National Register of Historic Places and is under the jurisdiction of the National Park Service.

Half King's Rocks is the site where Washington and the Mingo chief *Tanacharison* joined forces on the night of May 27, 1754, just before attacking the French force in the inaccessible glen which was to become known as Jumonville Glen.

The reason *Tanacharison* was called a "half king" is a subject of debate. The title had no meaning to the Iroquois, and so some have proposed that it was the British who decided to take away his kingship. They started to refer to him as the Half King perhaps because they only regarded him as merely a spokesman for his village, rather than for his entire tribe. On the other hand, they might have decided it was a more appropriate title after *Tanacharison* was subsequently ostracized by the Iroquois Confederacy. The Confederacy did so because he had violated their edict of neutrality in such flagrant ways. He found refuge at John Harris' home in Paxtang of Dauphin County, dying there of pneumonia on October 4, 1754.[66]

---

65. Ibid.
66. Christine Calvo, "A Half-King in America," *American Historical Manuscript Collection (AHMC)*, New York Historical Society, March 23, 2016.

L O C A T I O N : Half-King's Rocks are located in Jumonville Glen, between present-day Hopwood and Farmington, Fayette County, Pa, and seven miles west of Fort Necessity, 732 State Rt. 2021, Hopwood, PA 15445.

D D   G P S   C O O R D I N A T E S :
39°48'30.53" N -79°35'8.14" W

D R I V I N G   D I R E C T I O N S : Follow Route 99 South from Altoona, then bear right onto Route 22 West (exit #28). Continue on 22 West and then onto Route 119 Southwest through Uniontown. Follow onto Route 40 south to Jumonville Glen.

BIBLIOGRAPHY

Adomnan of Iona, William Reeves, editor, *The Life of St. Columba, Founder of Hy*, University Press for the Irish Archaeological and Celtic Society, Edinburgh, Scotland, 1857.

Bronner, Simon J., *Popularizing Pennsylvania, Henry Shoemaker and the Progressive Uses of Folklore and History*, Penn State University Press, University Park, PA, 1996.

Brooks, J. A., *Britain's Haunted Heritage*, Jarrold Publishing, Norwich, England, 1990.

Burl, Aubrey, *The Stone Circles of Britain, Ireland, and Brittany*, Yale University Press, New Haven, CT, 2000.

Carmer, Carl, *The Susquehanna*, Rinehart and Co., New York, 1955.

Cramer, Ben, *Hiking the Elk Trail, Plus the Fred Woods Trail*, Scott Adams Enterprises, Spring Mills, PA, 2016.

Day, Sherman, *Historical Collections of the State of Pennsylvania*, Ira J. Friedman, Port Washington, NY, 1843.

Donehoo, Dr. George P., *Indian Villages and Place Names in Pennsylvania*, Gateway Press, Baltimore, MD, 1977.

Donmoyer, Patrick, *Powwowing in Pennsylvania: Braucherei and the Ritual of Everyday Life*, Vol. IV of the Annual Publication Series of the Pennsylvania German Cultural Heritage Center at Kutztown University, 2018.

Dunn, Richard S. and Mary M., editors, *The Papers of William Penn, Volume 2*, University of Pennsylvania Press, Philadelphia, 1981.

Espenshade, A. Howry, *Pennsylvania Place Names*, The Evangelical Press, Harrisburg, PA, 1925.

Everts, Peck, and Richards, *History of that Part of the Susquehanna and Juniata Valleys, Embraced in the Counties of Mifflin, Juniata, Perry, Union and Snyder, in the Commonwealth of Pennsylvania*, Everts, Peck and Richards, Philadelphia, 1886.

Fisher, Forest K., *It Happened in Mifflin County*, Book 2, Mifflin County Historical Society, Lewistown, PA, 2005.

Grumet, Robert S., *Northeastern Indian Lives, 1632-1816*, University of Massachusetts Press, Amherst, MA, 1996.

Heckewelder, Reverend John, *History, Manner, and Customs of the Indian Nations*, Lippin-
    cott's Press, Philadelphia, 1876.
Hodge, Frederick Webb, ed., *Handbook of American Indians North of Mexico*, The Smith-
    sonian Institution, Bureau of American Ethnology Handbook of American Indians,
    Washington, DC, 1912.
Ignoffo, Mary Jo, *Captive of the Labyrinth: Sarah L. Winchester, Heiress of the Rifle Fortune*,
    University of Missouri Press, Columbia, MO, 2010.
Imhof, John D., *Elk County—A Journey Through Time, Volume One*, Baumgratz Publish-
    ing, St. Marys, PA, 2019.
Ingram, John H., *The Haunted Homes and Family Traditions of Great Britain*, Reeves and
    Turner Co., London, 1905.
Irving, Washington, *The Life of George Washington*, John Murray, London, 1856.
Jones, Richard, *Haunted Britain and Ireland*, New Holland Publishers, London, 2003.
Jones, Uriah J., *History of the Early Settlement of the Juniata Valley*, Telegraph Press, Har-
    risburg, PA, 1889.
Loudon, Archibald, *Loudon's Indian Narratives*, A. Loudon Press, Carlisle, PA, 1808.
McKnight, W. J., *Pioneer Outline History of Northwestern Pennsylvania*, Lippincott Com-
    pany, Philadelphia, 1905.
Melton, J. Gordon, *Religious Celebrations*, ABC-CLIO publishing, New York, 2011.
Merrill, James H., *Into the American Woods, Negotiators on the American Frontier*, Norton
    and Co., New York, 1999.
Montgomery, Thomas L., editor, *Frontier Forts of Pennsylvania*, Pennsylvania Historical
    Commission, Harrisburg, PA, 1916.
Myers, Albert Cook, *Narratives of Early Pennsylvania, West New Jersey, and Delaware 1630-
    1007*, Charles Scribner's Sons, New York, 1912.
Peck, George, D. D., *Wyoming; Its History, Stirring Incidents, and Romantic Adventures*,
    Harper and Brothers, New York, 1858.
Pritts, J., *Mirror of Olden Time Border Life*, Denny, Reynolds and Gehr Press, Abingdon,
    VA, 1849.
Raber, Paul and Verna Cowin, editors, *Foragers and Farmers of the Early and Middle Wood-
    land Periods in Pennsylvania: Recent Research in Pennsylvania Archeology Number 3
    (PHMC – 2001)*, Penn State University Press, University Park, PA, 2001.
Pollard, Albert F., contributor to the *Dictionary of National Biography*, Smith, Elder, and
    Co., London, 1900.
Sipe, C. Hale, *The Indian Chiefs of Pennsylvania*, Ziegler Printing Co., Butler, PA, 1927.
———, *The Indian Wars of Pennsylvania*, The Telegraph Press, Harrisburg, PA, 1931.
Smith, James, *An Account of the Remarkable Occurrences in the Life and Travels of Colonel
    James Smith*, John Bradford, Lexington KY, 1799.
Thwaites, Tom, *50 Hikes in Central Pennsylvania*, Countryman Press, Taftsville, VT, 2001.
Toy, Sidney, *Castles—Their Construction and History*, W. Heineman, London, 1939.
Wallace, Paul A. W., *Indians in Pennsylvania*, Pennsylvania Historical Commission, Har-
    risburg, PA, 1970.
———, *Indians Paths of Pennsylvania*, Pennsylvania Historical Commission, Harrisburg,
    PA, 1965.

Waterman and Watkins, *History of Bedford, Somerset, and Fulton Counties, Pennsylvania*, Waterman and Wakins, Chicago, 1884.

Weslager, Charles A., *The Delaware Indians: A History*, Rutgers University Press, New Brunswick, NJ, 1972.

White, Thomas, *The Witch of the Monongahela*, History Press, Charlestown, SC, 2020.

Withers, Alexander Scott, *Chronicles of Border Warfare*, Joseph Israel Publishing, Clarksburg, VA, 1831.

ABOUT THE AUTHOR

JEFFREY R. FRAZIER was born and raised in Centre Hall, Centre County, where he says he grew up in a "Tom Sawyer sort of way", later graduating with a BS from Penn State in 1967, and then with an MBA from Rider University in New Jersey in 1978. Some of the fondest memories of his boyhood include explorations of out-of-the-way spots in the mountains and accounts of the legends that seem to cling to them, and beginning in 1970 he began collecting those same kind of anecdotes from all over the state; ranging from the Blue Mountains of Berks and Lehigh Counties, the South Mountains of Adams County, the "Black Forest" area of Potter and Tioga Counties, the Alleghenies of Clearfield and Blair Counties, and the other counties in the middle. He has compiled his vast collection of tales into a series titled *Pennsylvania Fireside Tales*. The *Pennsylvania Mountain Landmarks* series is a continuation of his work, written in a format that the average reader can enjoy, especially those who love the green valleys and cloud-covered mountain peaks of Pennsylvania as much as he does.